Eungedup

a wetland summer diary

Giles Watson

First published 2026 by
FREMANTLE PRESS

Reprinted 2026.

Fremantle Press Inc. trading as Fremantle Press
PO Box 158, North Fremantle, Western Australia, 6159
fremantlepress.com.au

Copyright © Giles Watson, 2026

The moral rights of the author have been asserted.

This book is copyright. Apart from any fair dealing for the purpose of private study, research, criticism or review, as permitted under the *Copyright Act*, no part may be reproduced by any process without written permission. Every reasonable effort has been made to seek permission for quotations contained herein. Please address any enquiries to the publisher.

Cover design and illustration by Dominique Sharp.

 A catalogue record for this book is available from the National Library of Australia

ISBN 9781760995171 (paperback)
ISBN 9781760995188 (ebook)

Fremantle Press is supported by the Western Australian State Government through the Department of Cultural Industries, Tourism and Sport.

Fremantle Press respectfully acknowledges the Whadjuk people of the Noongar nation as the Traditional Owners and Custodians of the land where we work in Walyalup.

Eungedup

a wetland summer diary

Giles Watson

The natural flow of water sustains aquatic ecosystems that are central to our spirituality, our social and cultural economy and wellbeing. The rivers are the veins of Country, carrying water to sustain all parts of our sacred landscape. The wetlands are the kidneys, filtering the water as it passes through the land.

Nelson, Godden & Lindsay, *A Pathway to Cultural Flows in Australia*, 2018.

↓

This book was written on Menang Noongar boodja.
The author acknowledges that sovereignty was never ceded.

Contents

Map: Eungedup 7
A Note on Placenames and Noongar Words 8
Prelude 11
Kambarang 29
Map: Eungedup – The Northwest Wetland 31
Birak 49
Map: Maringup Creek – Southernmost Wetland 51
Map: Lake Saide 119
Map: Flow of the Eungedup Waters 129
Bunuru 181
Djeran 225
Map: Northwesternmost Wetland – Extent of Standing Water 243
List of Species 262
Acknowledgements 268

Legend

Standing water			Bare mud
Meadow drain, dry			Bare sand
Meadow drain, wet			
Reedbeds			Significant tree
Grasses, sedges, rushes			Woodland (mostly Peppermint)
Marri-Yate woodland			Juniper Myrtles
Road			Fox's earth
Path or track			
Old farm shed		**2.**	Place or sighting mentioned in text

A Note on Placenames and Noongar Words

Eungedup (pronounced Yoon-jed-up) is the Menang Noongar name for the body of water that appears on maps as *Lake Saide* (pronounced to rhyme with "shady"). Throughout this text, I have used *Eungedup* to refer to the whole of the wetland complex, and *Lake Saide* to refer specifically to the lake on the left-hand side of Browns Road as one enters from the north. Lake Saide was the body of water into which the surrounding wetland used to be drained for agricultural purposes.

Maringup Creek is the most southerly of the three wetland areas. It is more an area of sodden land and open water than a typical creek. This is also a Menang Noongar name.

The third wetland area, to the right of Browns Road, does not have a name of its own, or perhaps it was the original Eungedup. Readers can assume that I am writing about this area when Maringup Creek or Lake Saide are not specified in the text. I often refer to it as the Northwest Wetland.

Scotsdale Brook is, according to Google Maps, the name of the drain that feeds into and empties out of Lake Saide. It has been used here for convenience, although people who have long known the landscape simply call it "the drain."

Kinjarling is the Noongar name for Albany.

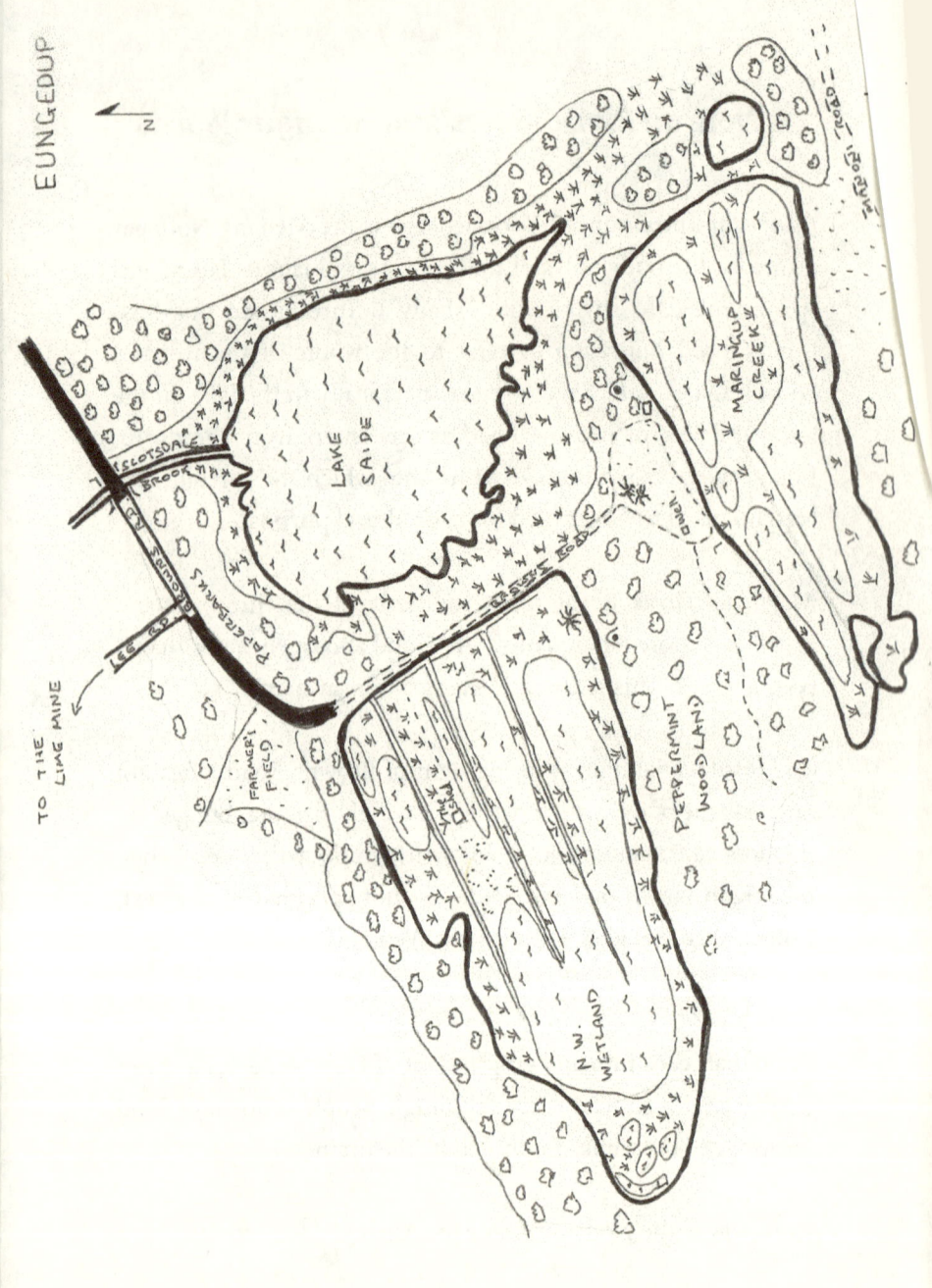

Porongurup is the mountain range immediately to the north of Kinjarling. *Koi Kyeunu-ruff*, known to the colonisers as the Stirling Range, is beyond them. These mountain ranges are full of places of sacred significance to Noongar people, and Koi Kyeunu-ruff is one of the most florally biodiverse ecosystems on the planet.

Yandjet is the Noongar word for plants in the genus *Typha*, known variously in the English language as *Reedmace* or *Bulrush*. I have used Yandjet throughout, except in cases where Reedmace performs an alliterative function, but when a single syllable word was required, I have simply used *reeds*. *Yanjidi* is the name for the plant's edible root.

The *Wagyl* is a gigantic snake from the time of the Dreaming whose movements across the landscape created watercourses and threw up hills and mountains. The Wagyl features frequently in Noongar oral traditions relating to specific places throughout southwestern WA.

This book makes use of Noongar names for the seasons, out of respect for the traditional owners of this land, and also because they help an observer to make more sense of changes in the yearly climate than traditional European season names. They are:

Birak (approximately December and January), the hot, dry season, when reptiles emerge from hibernation;

Bunuru (approximately February and March), the hottest season of the year, when seasonal water begins to dry up;

Djeran (approximately April and May), the beginning of cooler weather, when *Banksia* trees begin to flower;

Makuru (approximately June and July), the beginning of the rains, when the swans are moulting;

Djilba (approximately August and September), the season of wet days and clear, cold nights, when Cockatoos eat the Marri nuts;

Kambarang (approximately October and November), the season of receding rains, when the wildflowers appear.

Prelude

I need a Place where I can breathe – but after eighteen years abroad, I'm blocked at the trachea. I feel I am claimed by a different Place entirely – that I'm still subsisting on the final breaths I took there – a world's width away. Chronic fatigue drags me down, dries out my mouth, elongates every duty into drudgery. My dreams are haunted by constriction – a slow, parched throttling of the soul. No matter what medical solutions I may find, nothing within me can heal without this connection – even though this land is not my land, but another's.

I need a Place whose struggle is my struggle – a Place which floods and parches as I do – even though I am a newcomer to it. A liminal Place – for a liminal spirit. A Place open to receive the one who does not belong – a Place which is always open to receiving.

I do not want to own this Place. But I do want to be owned by it. I will come to it – I promise – knowing I am an interloper, hoping to be known.

I found a grove of coastal Karri trees five minutes from the beach – ringing with the songs of birds – and thought it might be the Place. But they cut down a corner of the grove to make way for a house, and the birds went silent.

I found a meadow beside the harbour spangled with astonishing constellations of flowers – and thought this might be the Place.

But they overturned the soil, poured concrete, built houses on the meadow, and the flowers dimmed and straggled.

I found a hillside covered with orchids overlooking a beach with a buried shipwreck – a Place where I felt I could see the spirits of ancestors not my own looking out between the leaves of Peppermints at a sailing ship taking on water from the spring – and thought this might be the Place. But they designated a corner of the hillside for a tourist resort – and it seemed the spirits scattered.

There is talk of a Place called Eungedup – half an hour by road from Kinjarling. I do not even know yet how to pronounce it – but it is said that there are Bitterns. I've heard rumours of a community initiative to buy it – restore and preserve it – so that no sentence will ever be written about Eungedup that begins with "But they...".

Eungedup – land of waters. This may be the Place.

I must go there. I must go without delay.

12 July 2022
Lake Saide, eastern shore

Australasian Bittern?
(Botaurus poiciloptilus?)

Before they gouged a road here
the only tracks were left by Roos.
On the wild side of the lake
I trace their quaggy trails
to reach the reeds.

Old *Banksias* form a grove here -
grizzled twigs festooned
with spiders' webs and fluff
of windblown seeds.

Frogs click and craik and rattle.

It's a warm day for winter
so I'm braving ticks and snakes
to see the open water.
Swamp Harriers reconnoitre
and hidden birds
make ghost noises.

I almost failed
to heed you - but here
I swear you're calling
like darker thoughts

or undertones of loss -
broad brown Bittern pulsing
your feathered resonance
in winter when the textbooks
insist that you are silent.

I guess but never see you
skygazing to align
striations with the reeds
invisible in plain sight -
straight and living pattern
of sunward growth and bronzing -
one of two thousand
remaining in Australia.

When your calls subside -
a great while I remain
to heed your silence
and other distant booms
from roads whose makers
barely seem to care
if this voiceless absence
should last forever -
who'd let weeds corrode
your precious wetland -
leach poisons into it -
steal its water.

Surely, we could save it -
if we ratchet up our hoping
but governments won't -
and councils won't -
and so you're waiting -
and I am gone to ground
beneath a *Banksia*.

When I wake
you've waded further -
and I fantasise a world
rejuvenated - where wetlands
flourish and Warblers' songs
are almost deafening - where
reeds and windless surface
quiver at your booming.

Later on at home I wonder -
could I have really heard you
at daytime and in winter
when your last thought is of breeding
and your heart is set on fishing
and on fattening in hope
of lustful summer - but I have you
on a recording - and compare you
obsessively with soundbites
of other dwindling Bitterns
across Australia - and find myself
not wishful - but convinced -
then tell myself I'm wrong -

that perhaps you were only
a Swamphen pumping up
his purple breast and drumming.

But it's enough. The wetland and its calling
swells within my dreaming - and I'm longing
to be walking - even wading - through
the humming summer of Kambarang
Birak and Bunuru - seeking living treasure
at Eungedup - place for sustained pilgrimage
where snakeskins - Bitterns' feathers -
shells of Dragonfly nymphs - birds'
splayed footprints up and down the silt -
emptied skins of Cicadas part way up
the Peppermints - bristling cones of *Banksias* -
eyegleams of the *Antechinus* -
the splash and spreading wake of the Rakali
are the relics - and the lip of land
at the edge of lapping water
where I can sit and get my notebook muddy
                                        is a shrine.

2 August 2022
At home

I have made my own donation toward the purchase of Eungedup by the Wilson Inlet Catchment Committee – a venture which will permanently ensure the preservation of the wetland's biodiversity. It is not an enormous amount – but it is enough of a bite out of my finances that I will need to be frugal for a couple of months. Today, I hear that ten percent of the required total has been raised. As it seeks donations, the Catchment Committee has chosen the Australasian Bittern as its flagship species for advertising the significance of the wetland. It appears on all their publicity materials, including the bumper sticker. This is not surprising, given that the still-decreasing population across Australia is only about two and a half thousand individual birds, and they have declined by seventy percent since the 1970s. But a flagship species is only the most charismatic representative of the hundreds or even thousands that contribute their lives to the thriving of a biodiversity hotspot, and I know from a single visit that Eungedup is positively heaving with life, much of it rare and endangered. A mining company has constructed a road that goes straight past it. Now is the time – or never. The loss of a precious wild space has already happened to me more than once since my arrival at Kinjarling in 2013: a quarter of a beloved little grove of Karri trees in Goode Beach has been felled to make way for a corrugated tin house, and a sensationally glorious wildflower site at Rushy Point, home to five different species of trigger plant, has been flailed to the ground and marked out in housing lots.

In one corner of a Field
I watched Extinction come -
a Meadow churned up by the Plough -
the Trigger Plants - all gone -

ruptured Soil let in the Weeds
so Sundews died - of Shade -
the felling of an Ancient wrought
a Desert - of a Glade -

Extinction came and stripped the Beetles
from the tops - of Trees -
and in the little Garden - caused
a Vanishing - of Bees -

and when - in hope of Moths - I left
a lonely outside Light -
nothing came - but Emptiness -
that deepened - like the Night.

They disappeared - by Increments -
a little Less - each Year -
though Trigger Plants live Elsewhere - yet -
they never will grow - here -

Time and again, on opposite sides of the world, I have seen wildernesses maimed, and have walked away bereft. I have grown weary, too, of the rhetoric: the wildlife will be "relocated", as if it were possible to simply shift a possum or a bird of prey without encroaching on the territory of another – as if it were possible to relocate the fungi and the bacteria in the soil which form the fundamental foundations of every wild and teeming space. I have begun to be afraid to *have* a favourite place at all, since my love for them seems to be a jinx which ensures their destruction. Either that, or it's just that wild places everywhere are under savage attack, and no matter which place a person chooses to adore, the relationship will end in mourning.

Donating money for the conservation and restoration of wilderness at Eungedup was nothing much, I have realised. The really dangerous investment has been allowing myself to love a wild space and hope, one more time, for its perpetual flourishing.

I need to share it with someone.

19 December 2022

Northwest Wetland (Browns Road entrance)

I walk here with my friend in silence
holding aloft a voice recorder - catching
calls I cannot yet identify - songs of plangent
wetness - tentative probings into sound -
passionate peepings - clucks and chatters -
swelling resonant utterances of frogs.

My friend has told me that she would need to take magic mushrooms to achieve the heightened state of consciousness that is triggered instantly and unbidden in me by the slant of light through gumleaves, or the glimpse of a dragonfly's wing. I grew up an only child, and with no sisters or brothers with whom I could compare my experience, always thought that this chemically unassisted, entirely legal high was normal, but she says that most people only find the vibrancy through the use of seriously intoxicating hallucinogens. And I, who can be sent tripping just by looking very closely at the way the soft strands of a feather hold together, am surrounded here by stimuli that could easily send me skyward.

A flock of Carnaby's Cockatoos traverses
with cries that seem to etch the sky
with echoes - and as the water - thick
with writhing tadpoles - wells about
my wellingtons - I feel it welling up
within me also - wildness and the wild swift
adoration - solitude not solitude but

obliteration of every human scheme
in the hemmed-in sap-green texture
of the reeds.

    I have not dared to feel this
for what seems like an aeon - this quiet
elation - this shedding of self and all concerns -
as songs of Reed Warblers lift the cold leaden
burden of being human in this remorseless
age of extinction. For here is no extinction -
only teeming. I shuffle through puddles
afraid to tread on Tadpoles - contrite that I
must ruffle surfaces or stir a cloud of mud.

I feel my eyes grow wide with watching - my ears
attuned to frequencies they had forgotten -
and everything that lives and breathes and
has ever lived and breathed is here - here -
here in Eungedup - breathing again through
stomata - gills - spiracles or lungs - and I
who had forgotten how ever to inhale
am given breath. I turn to see my friend
who perhaps for the first time sees me truly alive.

31 May 2023

At home

Today, the Wilson Inlet Catchment Committee announced that, with the help of BirdLife Australia, the Denmark Bird Group and the Gondwana Link, it has raised all the funds required to purchase Eungedup.

Somehow - as the idea in me was growing
for once the humans loved enough to do it -
pooling their resources - digging deep into pockets
to buy the wetland as the miners dug the pristine
sands of Nullaki beyond it. An old potato farm -
now reflooded and reverted to quivering wildness -
home of Bitterns - Crakes - Sandpipers - Harriers -
will never again come under plough - or be drained
for a road or factory or housing estate - or be mined
for anything
    other
        than
            Wonder -
a place where frogs
would pile on frogs
would pile on other
frogs - their soft bodies
a slurry in the water
at the bases of the reeds
and their calls would
seem to echo the place's
ancient name -

Eungedup -
    Eungedup -
        Eungedup -
            Eungedup -

27 August 2023
At school and at home

Chronic fatigue is getting the better of me. I am barely making it through my days at school. My students, especially my Literature group, are just about keeping me afloat. Sometimes, we take time out of a lesson to walk down to the estuary, hoping to see an Osprey taking a fish out of the water. The students have been reading the poems of Isabel Galleymore and Mary Oliver, and they are approaching wild things with a new reverence. I find one of them crouching on the shore, staring at something in a puddle of briny water. It is a Sea Snail, its tentacles out, leaving a trail through the sand. She tentatively pokes a finger at it. The tentacles withdraw, and she looks annoyed with herself. She apologises to the Snail: "Sorry I disturbed you. Please come out again." This lifts my spirits, even though the effort to walk back to the classroom is like wading waist-deep in estuarine mud.

By every recess time, I am feeling an overwhelming urge to go outside, lie on the grass under the sun and the clouds, and sleep for a very long while. Piles of marking await me, yet by the end of the day, I can scarcely summon the energy to pick up a pen. Sometimes, when I stand up, there is a swirl of nausea, and I lie back down, pinned to the sofa. I find myself writing stanzas which have the look of Emily Dickinson poems I am teaching in class but are really attempts to exorcise my symptoms.

Pale exhaustion made me lie
with clouds - across my gaze -
sunlight made them dissipate
like threads teased out - of gauze -

vanishing into a Sky
so vast - it drowned my mind -
and every thought I ever had
was scorched - in solar Wind

and in that Blue - at last beheld
with Eye - the end - of I -
I watched a World - evaporate -
in depths that swallowed - me

I have asked to take my long service leave in the final term of the year, hoping it will give me the time I need to make at least some sort of recovery. The fatigue comes in waves, but there are lulls in it, and during these, I hear more and more the call of Eungedup. Slowly, an idea dawns on me: on days when I am not pinned to the horizontal, I could while away some hours at the wetland, observing and writing. Simply being present in that place would be a healing grace, even if I just slump against a Peppermint tree when I get there, and watch the open water.

Eungedup is closed to the public, so I write to Shaun Ossinger, the Executive Officer of the Wilson Inlet Catchment Committee, seeking permission "to enter the site and explore it in solitude for a few days" during my long service leave. As I am writing the email, the idea seems to grow in proportion, dawning on me like a vision:

> I would propose to spend some whole days there, arriving by dawn and leaving after sunset, perhaps augmented with some additional, shorter trips. I would, of course, take nothing but notes, photographs and sound recordings, and treat the site and its flora and fauna with the utmost respect. I would be prepared to park my car somewhere on Lake Saide Road and walk down Browns Road to gain access, rather than driving anywhere near the site. My explorations would need to be solitary in order for me to fully immerse myself in the place.

By the time I click the "send" button, I feel as though my heart is kedged to the proposal. I find myself compulsively checking my inbox for a reply. A refusal would be like drowning.

28 August 2023
At school

There is a motivational speech for the children in the school assembly. It is heartfelt and beautiful, and it is drawn from personal experience of suffering and hardship, but it is about learning to "flip" your attitude when you feel like you are going under. I feel too drained to sit upright in a chair, so I have sat down on the floor of the gymnasium with my back to the wall so that the cool of the concrete will keep me awake, wondering how I go about "flipping" my response to my current condition. There is a scrap of paper and a stub of pencil in my pocket. I take them out and write, leaning forward against my knee:

There are things I cannot - Flip -
their Load is too far - Down.
Optimism - perishes -
fortitude is - Gone -

my Mettle - made of Feathers
flounders under - Weight -
Gravity snaps both my Legs -
so then what hope - in Flight?

Somehow, I dredge up the strength to get through the rest of the day, helped by the warmth I feel from my students when I walk into the classroom. After school, I log on to my email. There is a message from Shaun, confirming that I can visit Eungedup as often as I like over the summer. For a fleeting moment, my spirits leap. But it is more than half an hour's drive from my home in Kinjarling to Eungedup, and my proposal to spend whole days at the wetland, written only yesterday, seems hopelessly optimistic. My hope is fluttering on the ground like a wounded bird.

Kambarang

Legend

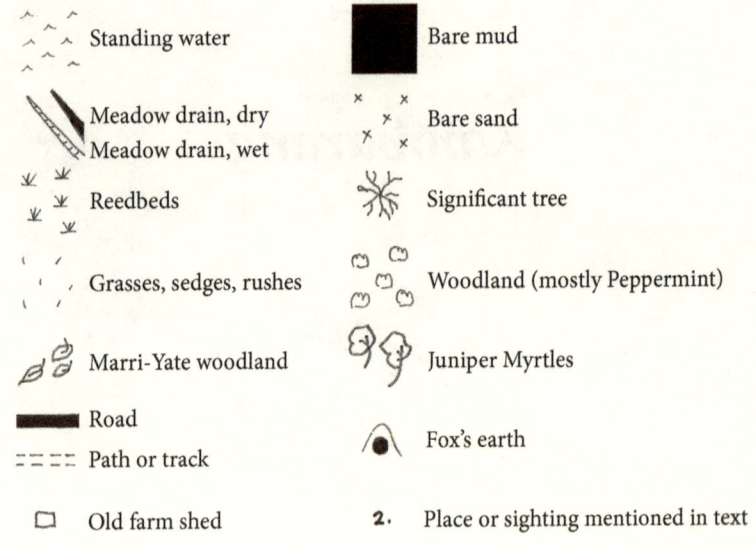

Northwest Wetland: Key to sightings marked on the map

1. Observation "Chapel" 3: Reed Warbler, Swamphen, Spotted Crake, Spoonbills. A grassy path leads to The Shed from here.
2. Observation "Chapel" 2: Spotted Crake, Spotless Crake, Buff-Banded Rail, Swamphen.
3. Observation "Chapel" 3: Reed Warbler, Fairywrens, Inland Thornbill, Grassbird. 4. is also viewed from here.
4. Large *Banksia* tree. Sometimes a perch for a Swamp Harrier.
5. Tiger Snake observed hunting. The snakes are throughout the area, on land and in the water, and regularly cross Browns Road.
6. Wood Sandpiper, and various other waders, ducks and pelicans.
7. White-Necked Heron.
8. Shelducks regularly fly over here toward Lake Saide.

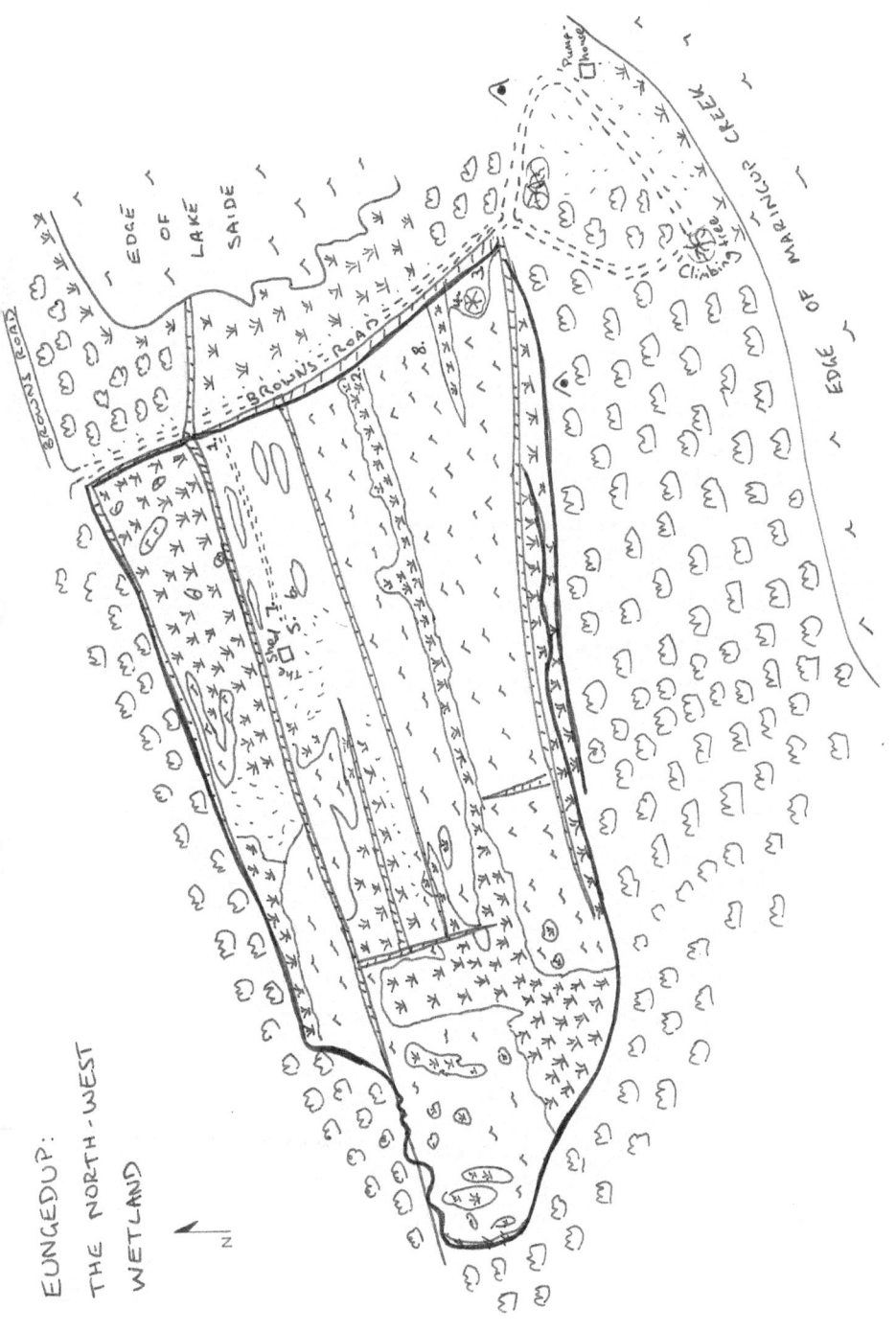

4 October 2023

Northwest Wetland (Browns Road entrance)
2.30 p.m. to 4.30 p.m.

In Kambarang, the snakes awaken. Birds build nests, stoke themselves up and sit awaiting hatching – then run themselves thin and ragged among the sun-coloured flowers of *Acacias* and *Hibbertias*, catching insects for their nestlings. Orchids rise up, imitating wasps and flies – sundews twine and flower – Trigger Plants slap Bees upon their bottoms. There is a last, delicious flush of wetness before the dry of summer – the wetland's belly swelled and fecund. Nymphs of Dragonflies climb up stems and trunks. Swallows dabble mud, swoop across the waters, daub their nests and chitter. Fresh shoots of Yandjet, or Reedmace, catch the wind and flutter.

Shaun has invited me to meet him at Eungedup in the early afternoon. He will be busy with a group of researchers, but he can spare a little time to talk with me about safety considerations, and about where the motion-detection cameras have been positioned for capturing images of the fauna, so that, if I am taken short, I don't make the mistake of peeing in front of one of them. He is pleased I am wearing wellington boots, and asks that I always wear them, or a pair of protective gaiters, because the wetland is riddled with venomous Snakes. I agree to send him a text message every time I arrive at Eungedup, and another every time I depart, since while I am there, I am under the Catchment Committee's duty of care. The researchers clearly have much to do, and, perhaps, the excitement of being back here has given me an added ration of strength, so I wander off on my own up Browns Road while they are working.

I have a small, purple and gold, ornate notebook with me, decorated with an Andrew Lang fairy design. Perhaps the researchers think I cut a strange figure, wading off by myself down the flooded track, with my eyes flitting between this notebook, the reedbed and the sky.

The way into Eungedup is down a rust-coloured road
between Peppermints and Paperbarks. In springtime
there are flaring petals of yellow *Hibbertias*
and low *Acacias* afire with spines - flecking undergrowth
with saffron. Where water floods roots of Paperbarks
Rattling Froglets weave a textured chorus - a wet weft
of versicle and response - amid glimpses of Yandjet
through trees - casting their seeds to the wind.
A Raven twists in air. His voice turns with him -
so my eye is drawn upward by his flight - I see
the lower twigs of Paperbarks are wearing heavy beards
of well-fluffed Yandjet seeds. These darker trees
open out into sunlit Juniper Myrtles - mostly boles -
tufted canopies an afterthought to trunk. Rustling reeds
and Grasshopper-charms - a lone Silvereye dangling
her strung charm of wistfulness out in sky -
floating motes of birdvoice drifting and remote.

Five human researchers are standing gumbooted
wearing rubber gloves - preparing for taking samples

as if at a crime scene - or perhaps - one jokes -
dealing with a biohazard. "*We're* the biohazard,"
I say - and luckily they laugh - my way of breaking ice.
Shaun has almost stepped on a Dugite -
reminds me next time to bring a bandage.

We're here on sufferance where Snakes are apex.

I wander on and leave them among mud and water
where the greening wetness laps against the trunks.

Both sides of Browns Road are hedged with reeds
flowering at above the height of a human head.
A Musk Duck resonates beyond. His wet voice
is like a water droplet when it swells and stretches
tension before falling into a deep and ferny well.
He has distilled all the plops and slops of open water
into one fat droplet which he tosses from his throat.
A break in the reeds. Swallows and Martins whisk
over - preceding a flock of fifteen White Ibises
making themselves scarce where a Sea Eagle soars.
I am standing still enough that Froglets rattle
at my feet while Egrets - gravely concentrating -
tread the edge of a far-off gleam of water.
Out there also a Swan opens pinions above
where she glides upon the surface - white tips
edging black wings above the white tumult
the wind is raising. Some black bird flies too fast
to know a name for her - but in her bill she carries
a clump of seeds of Yandjet carefully gathered.

The buff-white frazzle of Yandjet seeds
is like the heavy-felted guzzle of the Froglets -
texturing twigs - texturing grass stems -
texturing nests - weaving with songs of Warblers -
weaving soil with air with water with touch and sound.
Now there's a Heron beside the Egret - two more Swans -
beyond them - another bank of reeds with fluff
and seeds lifting into distance. On a grass leaf
a green Beetle with buff elytra - the whole creature
the size of the white moon under my little fingernail -
climbing - reaching the grass tip and turning
around. A spit of rain. I turn and follow the golden zazz
of a Dragonfly back down the road. Female Dragonflies
bend their abdomens under leaves where the way
is waterlogged - some upheld by males - some alone -
flying - stopping - depositing in the green growth
at the centre of the track where Tadpoles wriggle
among grass stems and Bugs splay their legs to skate.

The researchers have syringes for catching water -
strange - this glimpse of plastic in the wild.
They're here collecting and detecting DNA - forcing
wetland water through a filter - finding traces
left behind by anything that lives here - pauses
to drink here - flies above here - eats a meal here -
sleeps on a branch or metamorphoses on a stem
and leaves invisible deposits in the water -
everything that wades or wanders through - as I
am wandering - through -

                wishing I could never

                      leave a trace

                              of human DNA -

Shaun and the researchers need to take samples from the other end of the site, at the north side of Maringup Creek. They lurch off in the back of his four-wheel drive, while I wander contentedly far behind them.

Two light grey Cygnets glide the open water
within the safe V of their mother's wake
as a Swamphen pumps himself up - lets out
a resonant sneeze that shakes the reeds
and a Reed Warbler - invisible somewhere
among the trembling stems - extemporising
so inventively and so long I might have forgotten
to breathe - splashes rash notes out slapdash

as the mother Swan glides behind the reedbed
and for one lingering instant the Cygnets sit
amid the long nurturing glisten of her wake
as it plops against reed-stems - then follow -

26 October 2023
South side of Maringup Creek (Manoni Road entrance)
4.37 p.m. to 5.30 p.m.

There are two different routes which give access to Eungedup: Browns Road, which enters the wetland from the north, and Manoni Road, a track at the end of a red dirt road, often bone-shakingly corrugated, which leads to a small, raised, grassy area, surrounded by reeds and impenetrable scrub, to the south of the site, and not far from the ocean. There is very little walking to be done from the Manoni Road entrance – you simply wander down the lane, stand, and raise a pair of binoculars – but the whole of Eungedup stretches out before you. I have decided that it is a place I can visit when I am well enough to drive but am likely to be too depleted to walk on my arrival. Today is certainly one of those days. There is a radical disconnection between my emotional state, which is ebullient at the prospect of seeing the wetland from a higher trajectory, and the leaden weight which seems to tug me physically downward with every step. The ebullience in me wishes that I could stay for many hours, but my body will manage one at most.

I could stare for ages at the white flashes of Waterfowl in sunlight.

On the right-hand of the open water - a flotilla
of bobbing Coots are turning the white shields
of their faces into the wind - swivelling on paddle-toes
in water. Among them a single Hoary-Headed Grebe
is bobbing cootlike - his cheeks half-white - on water.

Two Black Ducks sail by - with not a touch
of whiteness on them - until one shifts in water
and a moment - in the sun - her cornea flashes white.
Five Shelducks veer up into the air from off the water -
bank and catch the sunlight on the stretched whiteness
of their shoulders. Two peel away below the level
of the reeds - three are banking right above me
with their wild white scapulae bright above the water.
Three shadowed Cygnets are losing their whiteness -
but white gleams on the red skin above the blunt bill
of the Pen their mother - where she catches it in sunlight
after dipping for the pondweed in the water.
Two Swamp Harriers are quartering the water
ringed about with white at the bases of their tails -
tipping into the whiteness of the sunlight over water -
and off the water a startled Cormorant has flushed -
her stark black silhouette a snake-necked answer
to the bright white I find is flashing on all things else
above the wind-caught, white-bedazzled water.

28 November 2023

*Northwest Wetland (Browns Road entrance)
to the north shore of Maringup Creek
8.50 a.m. to 2.07 p.m.*

The water has all dried up from the road -
those tadpoles now are frogs - the air crisp
with the songs of Cicadas. They seem to sing
in rhythm, their stridulations breathlike - pulsing -
woven with the whistles of birds - the atmosphere
textured with the flights of Flies. Below the heights
of the reeds and grasses - little Blues and Darts
are dancing. Every step sets off mass strafings
of straw-coloured Grasshoppers who disappear
as soon as they touch the stubble. At the edges
of the wetland, Damselflies dance - their places
taken - as I wander further in - by stouter Dragonflies -
aggressive predators who never rest. They quarter
their lands and clash with neighbours at the edges
of their ranges - in a perpetual state of hunting
and skirmish - except for when they couple
and everything turns delicate and tender - tandems
to the singing of the Warbler. Amid the reeds -
Motorbike Frogs are starting up and revving.

I step into a gap in the reeds and find a trackway
submerged in rotting vegetation - which I follow
'til I reach the open water where a White-Necked Heron
watches - on the verge of flight but waiting. A Wader -
cryptic-coloured - stops and opts for absolute stillness

in my presence. Harmless Flower Flies lurk
on fallen leaves - like wasps. Hungry Dragonflies
hawk above me. Five Pelicans flow overhead and soar.

I leave the Heron and the Wader to their watching -
fade into the reeds and back onto the road -
and make my way toward more distant open water -
the one place where Damselflies and Dragonflies
seem equally at home. Along my way I meet:

Western Xenica Butterflies
Geitoneura minyas

Xenicas the colour of dry summer dapples
flit in and out of shade
flashing out onto sunlit flowers
then flicking sideways - to hide.

This they achieve by closing their wings
and conjuring dryness of leaves -
their little domains strung out down the path -
kingdoms for mottle-winged Selves.

Xenicas - wending - occasionally meet
and batter each other with wings -
no lovelier battle ever was fought
in waltzes and flutterwinged songs.

I pass in ten paces a *Xenica*'s world -
pause watchful - then enter another

whose wing-spots are pinpoints - who flits into light
embodying Wind - and dry weather.

Tau Emerald
Hemicordulia tau

He battered past me on three-and-a-half wings.
Then faltered - and perched on a stick -
I leaned in to look at him clasping the bark
by the reeds at the edge of the track -

his eyes were a glaze of brownness and blue -
his thorax was banded with brown -
his segmented abdomen slimmed to a tip
swaying in wind - pointing down -

the edge of his cellophane tattered and torn -
he pivoted - cautious to fly -
but held them at ready - those other three wings -
sufficient - to bear him - away -

Mud-Dauber Wasp
Sceliphron sp.

The Dauber Wasp hovers - dissatisfied -
this mud is too dry - and will crumble.
She tests out a wetter patch - tasting the earth
and lands with her forewings atremble.

Her body articulates - needle-thin waist
lets her abdomen hang at an angle -
she bends till her eye-globes abut with the ground -
her six limbs splay out - and entangle.

Her forelegs and mandible scooping together
ball up the mud in a bundle.
Her wings blur like smoke - rising in air -
her body - a flickering candle -

Sand Wasp
Bembix sp.

Bembix the Sand Wasp - hunting for flies
to paralyse - store in a burrow
and feed to her little ones - basks on the sand
legs splayed the palest of yellow -

black her long body - banded with blue
shrouded with traceried wings -
she seems unassuming - no one could guess
how she homes in - and pounces - and stings.

Sun Moth
Synemon sp.

My eyes - are chasing Dragonflies
amid the drying grass -
when - there! A Flicker rises up -
flares - and disappears -

a Flame - in shroud of charcoal
I tremble - to disturb -
when something Incandescent
should wear a cloak - so drab.

Blue Skimmer Dragonfly
Orthetrum caledonicum

His fuselage of tarnished metal
rests upon dry grass
where he sits awhile - worn out
with wings splayed - like a Cross -

all the morning - he has flown
in tandem - with his Mate
to lower her down - on waterweeds
that leaf - amid the Wet.

It's worn him quite to powder
to carry her - with Care -
a flight of sunlit Ardour
that almost quenched - his Fire -

Fruit Flies
Euleia sp.

On diagonal edges perch the Flies
on long leaves of the reeds -
they sit with heads beyond the Edge
to know best - when to flee -

eye-globes have extensive view
of reed-shades - and the World -
with heads as large as abdomens -
six tiny feet - that hold -

and filamental wings at rest
their margins dipped in ink -
they sleep - they wake - with bulging orbs
like droplets - on the brink -

> Golden Grass Carpet Moth
> *Anochloris subochraria*

I find her where she fell - from flight
and stoop in grass - to read
the marks of ebbing swamp on sand
receding - down her wing.

She fed upon *Hibbertia*
growing - in that hollow -
shaped her wings like petals
and borrowed - from their Yellow -

could anybody kneel before
this grass stalk where she hangs
and fail to marvel? She reflects
her Habitat - in wings.

Grass-Dart Butterfly
Taractrocera sp.

Grass-Dart with barred antennae -
little shard - of Rust -
drinks a moment - from a Legume -
startles - and is lost -

lived a larval life - in grasses -
emerged - corroded Arrow -
glimpsing her tiny life
is Antidote - for sorrow -

⚹

Now I spend an hour knee-deep in open water
hoping for the damselflies to lose their fear
and hover closer - seeking half-submerged twigs
on which to rest their wings or mate. I lose motion -
still my breathing - calm my mind - and wait.

Red and Blue Damselfly
Xanthagrion erythroneurum

Red and Blue Damselfly - clasping a stem
of Yandjet fallen in water -
little black shades in your eyes of vermilion -
turquoise your tail-bands. I falter

to see you - electrical pulse
embodied in fizz-wings and segments.
Miniature lightning has fractured a jewel
and kindled a Life in this Fragment -

Blue Ringtail Damselfly
Austrolestes annulosus

Little flying Locomotive
with his blue caboose
parks himself - at reedy stations -
sets off - in a burst -

sees another - and is angry -
derails him - in midair -
lands again - through azure windshields
regards me - from afar -

I approach - so very slowly
afraid to cause him stress.
He waits - then flies - to his timetable -
Damselfly Express.

I walk back in the growing heat – reluctant to leave, but flagging. The day has settled into a somnolent hum and here and there on stems – Damselflies are hanging:

Slender Ringtail Damselfly
Austrolestes analis

If copper could have eyes and wings
and burnish - into Being -
she'd perch amid the shadows
where Paperbarks are growing

to watch the sinking Sun withdraw
its goldenness - from Sky -
until perhaps a Globe of Dew
took shape - upon her Eye -

Egg-laying Damselflies

I see a Wheel in air -
it kinks - into a Heart -
a Cycle of two living Beings
defying Wind - and Weight.

It trundles through the sky
fitful in its choice -
then lowers - settles on a Leaf
afloat amid - the Moist.

The Father holds the Mother up -
she concentrates on laying -
I turn away - I dare not watch
a Pulse away from drowning -

Birak

Legend

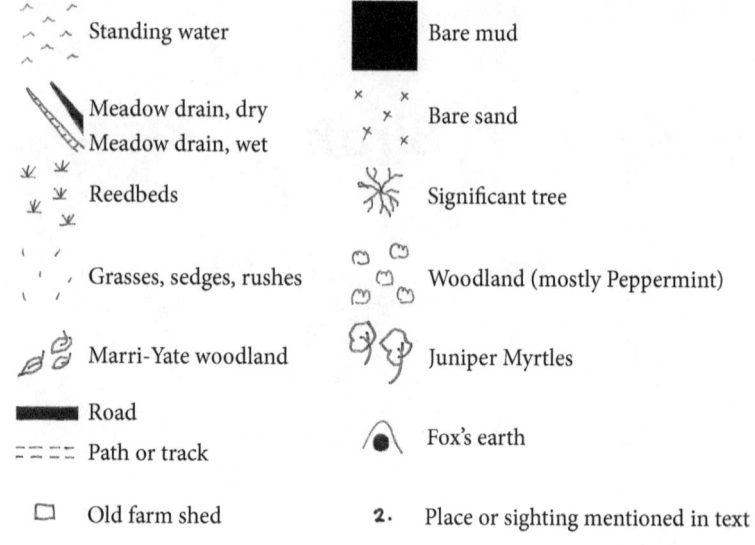

- Standing water
- Meadow drain, dry
- Meadow drain, wet
- Reedbeds
- Grasses, sedges, rushes
- Marri-Yate woodland
- Road
- Path or track
- Old farm shed
- Bare mud
- Bare sand
- Significant tree
- Woodland (mostly Peppermint)
- Juniper Myrtles
- Fox's earth
- 2. Place or sighting mentioned in text

Maringup Creek: Key to Sightings Marked on the Map

1. Climbing-Tree (a Peppermint)
2. Tiger Snakes hunting throughout this area.
3. Spotted Crakes
4. Sun Moth, Dragonflies, Sand Wasp
5. Immature Spotted Crake. Launching place for kayak.
6. Kingfisher sightings
7. Swamp Harrier eating prey
8. Roosting-trees

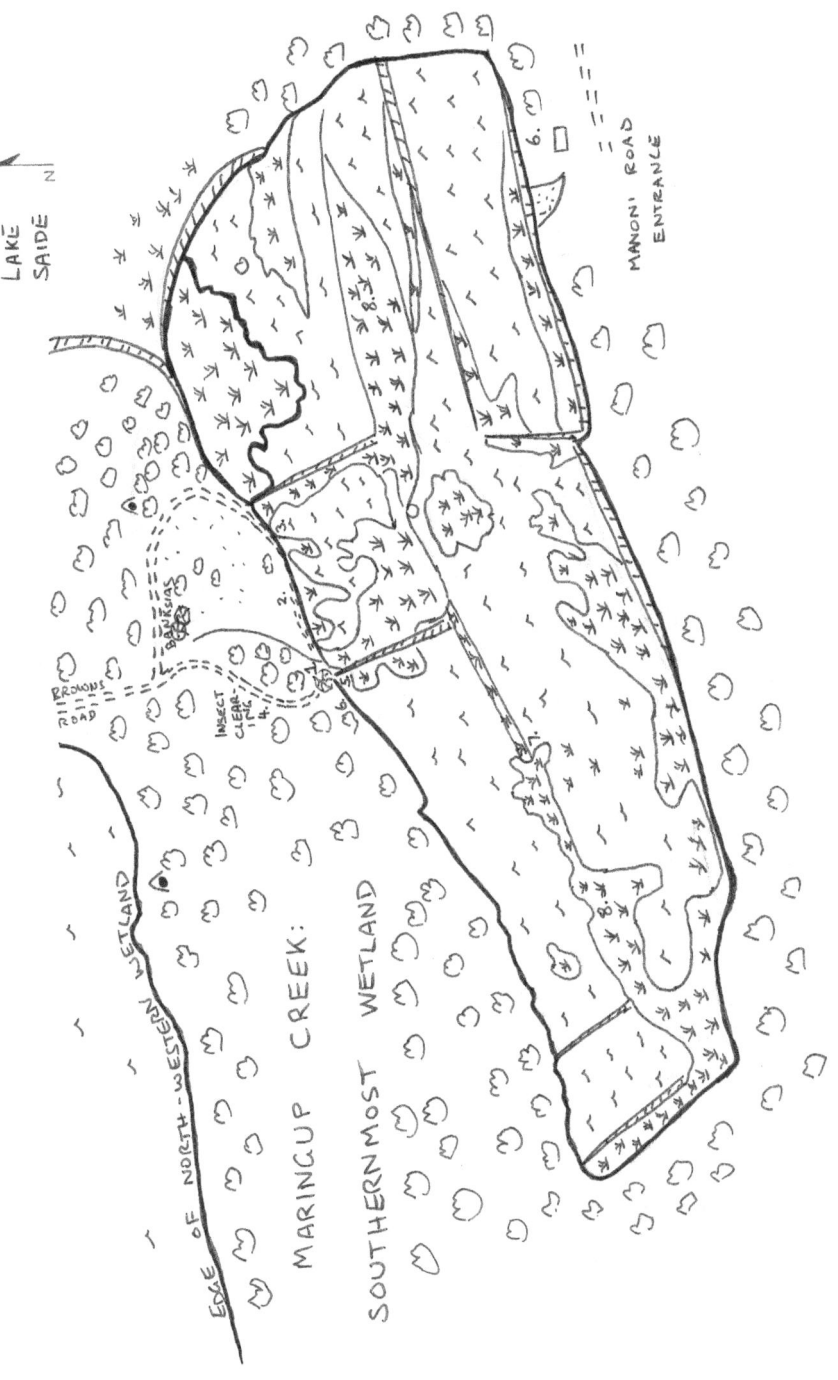

1 December 2023
At home

The Noongar season of Birak is the time when tadpoles, their legs grown underwater, their tails progressively absorbing into their backsides, begin to emerge on dry land and complete their transformations into tiny frogs. Fledgling birds take their first tentative flights from their nests – or are sometimes over-bold, and try to leave too early. Birak is the season of the young, the season when snakes rest a few days, their eyes clouding over, then snag their skins on twigs and peel them off, emerging glistening and renewed. But fatigue has struck me down again, my dismay compounded by the fact that my leave from school began in early October, and my condition has worsened, not improved.

A Sleep - steals upon me
that I - cannot resist -
it curbs - with its Bridle -
shudders me - to Rest -

it floors me - when my Joy - or Fear -
has reached its highest Ebb -
caresses - like the Feather -
or clouts me - with a Club -

it kills me - at a Canter -
a Tremor - through the Veins -
the Ghoul - astride the Saddle -
hauling - at the Reins -

I stumble - at the Apex -
shudder - at the Sun -
when my Heart - is Startled -
my Brain is set - to Stun -

I scour the internet looking for references to Eungedup, and trawl back through emails from the Wilson Inlet Catchment Committee. There are several which, in my haze of fatigue and desperation to complete my work at school, I had entirely missed. I re-read the triumphant email of 31 May 2023, when the Committee announced that it had raised all the funds required to buy the wetlands. Now, it is planning the next phase: in one corner of Eungedup, it will build an interpretive centre with a focus on engaging school students. There are no plans to build the usual boardwalks and bird hides. Instead, much less invasive plans are afoot: elevated, high-definition video cameras will provide live footage of goings-on in the wetlands, so that their natural inhabitants can carry on their lives undisturbed. It will be possible to watch this footage live in classrooms. Bird calls will be detected with electronic song meters, and special buoys will monitor the water quality.

But there are other, less pleasing developments. A mining company wants to clear an area of Peppermint woodland for a lime pit, less than a kilometre to the north-west of the edge of the wetland – seven hundred metres, in fact, from a nesting pair of Bitterns. Bitterns are highly sensitive to mining noise, and their breeding habits require comparative silence, so that females can hear the booming of the males. Lime exposed by the mining would be caught up in the wind and be blown across Eungedup, threatening its pH balance.

I snap my laptop closed, reeling. Repeatedly in the hours that follow, I suppress an urge to melt into tears, because I know that if I let myself cry, I will have difficulty in staunching the flow. I resist the urge to spiral into a misanthropic rage, and purge it with poetry.

I'm tired of being - a Human Being -
I wish I was - a Bird
clutching to - a flexing Stem
where the Rushes - bend -

I would sing - a sunlit Note -
cast Calumny - away -
Duplicity - could not - divide -
nor Apathy - destroy -

my Footprint - scarcely - leave a Mark -
Wingbeat - barely stir
a Turbulence - to turn a Leaf -
a Flit - obscure a Star -

3 December 2023

At home

I lie down on the Grass
too drained to really - Live
too stretched to pick a Pencil - up.
A Fantail - above
is tweaking insects in the tree
tilting - looking down
and cocking her Sagacious Head
as in my dressing gown
I wonder how I ever stood
or raised the will - to Be.
This Birak - she has laid three Eggs
and fledged - and flew - all Three.
She splays her waving Tail
in her Peppermint's green Crown -
I feel this bursting in my Head
and stir - to write it - down -

6 December 2023

Northwest Wetland (Browns Road entrance)
to the north shore of Maringup Creek
1.11 p.m. to 3.34 p.m.

I lie in bed for hours most mornings unable to move, longing for the wetlands. Often, I watch and re-watch footage I have taken on my mobile phone on previous visits – a poor substitute for being there on the ground. By lunchtime today, I have rallied a little. I now have a wooden crate set aside, which contains all the equipment for my visits: a pair of binoculars, identification guides for Birds, Dragonflies and Damselflies, a water bottle, sunscreen, mosquito-repelling substances, a warm beanie, a cool sunhat, a rolled-up waterproof coat, various snacks, a waterproof camera, and most importantly, snake-proof gaiters and a snakebite kit which straps onto my belt. There's a feeling of triumph when I carry it to the car.

On the dry land between the lakes
two *Banksia* trees are leaning
as if dancing - their limbs lifted
aloft - heavy with foliage. Beyond -
a patch of blackberries is fenced off
so goats can graze and help with weeding.
They pause their eating as I pass them -
hoping for more palatable fare than brambles.

The grass gives way to rushes where
white Moths flit and cling. Dragonflies scud.

Bird sounds lift from open water - spilling
songs of wetness onto drier ground.

Common Brown Butterfly
Heteronympha merope

The *Xenica*s - most are gone now
replaced by larger Browns
who float about the glade the same -
and lazy - bask their wings -

they close a blink - then open up
to flash four staring Eyes -
mottled - as the *Xenica*s -
yet twice the claim - for size.

One *Xenica* alone remains -
his lifeline quite - outstrung -
he flies about - in tatters -
the Sun shines - through his wing -

Blue-Spotted Hawkers
Adversaeschna brevistyla

Eye to eye with a Dragonfly
a moment in the Bog
I saw his compound eye up close -
the way he hung - a leg -

he glanced at me - I stared at him
I hoped a while - to stay -
a Dragonfly's prerogative
to sidle fast - away -

A Lycid Beetle on the wing
meets - a Dragonfly -
consumed in air - his carapace
a portion - dropping by -

then resting on a Peppermint -
reflections in her wings -
she catches Sky in spotted orbs
and like a Blossom - hangs -

The Musk Duck's Song

Plangent - as a dewfall -
Musk Duck - dropping notes -
contemplating - ripples -
interrupting - thoughts -

Movement of a reed leaf
signalling - a Wren -
she will stay - in shade for now -
emerge - when I am gone -

Harrier flies over -
brindle - flash of white -

Musk Duck goes silent
embodiment - of Wet -

Jewel Spider
Austracantha minax sp.

Launches out on filaments -
body clotted cream
spined about with ebony -
builds - where winds are calm -
a net of snares - to catch a moth -
and stitch up - in a shroud.
I lie down on the grass to see
her spin - against a Cloud -

Female Aurora Bluetail Damselfly
Ischnura aurora

An upright grass leaf lit by sun -
she seeks - and clasps its edge
moulds her body to its slope
and quells the flying urge -

Damselfly not longer than
a needle - wears the drape
of wings three-quarters of her length
and clings there - gazing - up -

tiny hairs upon her thorax -
hairs upon the leaf -
asleep perhaps - perhaps on watch
leaf-green and - aloof -

⚹

As I make my way from Eungedup, I stop to find the stream that feeds Lake Saide. Its banks are a tangle of weeds, but on a bare patch of soil, a Blue Skimmer Dragonfly is basking, and native Beetles climb the stems in this hinterland between the farmscape and the wild.

Two Red-Tailed Cockatoos cling to a Peppermint's highest branches. A Brown Falcon stoops to earth – talons clenching downward – rises unsuccessful – whirls up into wind.

In the distance, a Wedge-Tailed Eagle wheels over farmland – those teeming lakes all hidden behind their screens of trunks and quivering leaves.

10 December 2023
At home

There ought to be a whole library-full of psychological literature about Chronic Fatigue Syndrome, hypnagogic hallucinations, and genuine sleeping dreams. One day, when I have the energy, I will research it. For now, perhaps, it will be enough to record my own experience.

Currently, my hypnagogic hallucinations – vivid visions that occur somewhere in the hinterland between wakefulness and sleep – are heavily influenced by Damselflies. If I've been spending a long time in the garden weeding, my hypnagogia draws my mind to fractals which endlessly multiply the leaves and flowers of dandelions; now, it echoes Eungedup – somewhat strangely. There are lots of elongated bodies and diaphanous wings, and on the whole, I welcome them. If I cannot be physically in the wetland, then at least they are the kind of substitute that has all the benefits of inebriation without the hangovers or the embarrassment. I have no particular objection to being too dazed to interrupt – still less, interpret – the progression of a thousand different variations on the wings of a Damselfly.

But dreams – genuine sleeping dreams, and the hypnagogic state that lies on the *other* side of sleep – are another matter. I think my chronic fatigue grew out of a bout of glandular fever I never knew I had, but which turned up a couple of years ago on a blood test. Quite often, when I'm most debilitated, there is still a tenderness about the lymph nodes in my throat. When I am in an unconscious state, this sensation melds hideously with the memory of an experience of violent semi-strangulation which I experienced during a gratuitous assault, also just a few years ago. It resonates horribly with a deep-seated fear of constriction which I remember from my childhood, and with a darkly tolling fear that somehow I am responsible, and deserve it.

I feel a Leather compassing
about my bleeding Mind
and Someone drew the Buckle - in -
I cannot clutch - to mend -

I sense it hanging - like a Shroud
from the flexing Strap -
blinded by a Tightening
that never deigns - to Stop -

Tyrant of my screeching Soul
who blots - with stunning Light -
my holy Dark - in Negative -
searing into - White -

At other times, my nightmares return inexorably to that monotonously terrifying archetypal favourite, immortalised by Edgar Allan Poe in 'The Tell-Tale Heart', and by Emily Dickinson in her poem, 'I felt a funeral, in my brain'. To cut short an always agonisingly long and interminably varied story, somebody is trying to bury me alive, or failing that, to smother me under an overturned sofa.

I hid behind the Curtains -
he flushed me - into Sight -
I scampered down the Hallway -
invoked the Dark - of Night -

he blundered - into Tables -
I hid - behind a Chair -
he paused to light - a Lantern -
I was - no longer - There -

I hunched myself - beneath a Bed -
I felt the Mattress pitch -
I knew he sat above me now -
and kept a Spider's watch -

I heard his Pulse - I smelt his Rage -
his Incandescence - burned -
then he stood - astride my World -
my Darkness - overturned -

I wake up absolutely mortified, of course, with my pulse racing, and try desperately to re-induce the hypnagogic state which gave me Damselflies' bodies and wings stuck inside a kaleidoscope. *I'd rather be in the wetland*, I am thinking, and lie, and cannot move.

10 December 2023

*Northwest Wetland (Browns Road entrance),
west along the wooded north shore of Maringup Creek
10.45 a.m. to 1.11 p.m.*

Before the Peppermints close in
a solitary Magpie carols. Painted Ladies
splash themselves in shadows
and chase away the Browns.
Grey Fantails chatter under Paperbarks
and where a broken branch creaks
against another - Ravens call boylike -
the Cicada pulse grows louder.

As soon as I am alongside the reeds
I hear the Warbler and the Wrens
and fresher *Xenica*s are dancing.
A pair of Dragonflies flies past
in a heart-shaped crush that might
be mating - or a fight to the death.
Dry Grasshoppers and Crickets
rattle. Where there are no trees
the wind breaks in, stirring the Yandjet -
its inflorescences tilt like wands.
There are clucks and squawks
of hidden Swamphens - a Rosella
skimming over - and bubbling voices
I do not know. Tiny black Wasps
dig holes into the pathway - and
disappear inside them - into coolness.

A Fantail follows me - looping
from branch to branch - chattering
and posturing. I turn into the reeds -
part them with my fingers - gazing in -
and there - perfectly framed -
entirely placid - among old dead branches
a Swamp Harrier is perching -
staring out toward a squabbling
of Ducks - and beyond her - humps
of dunes - held together with green-grey
vegetation - sheltering the wetland
from the Sea. I retreat - let the long straps
of reed-leaves seal her off from sight.

Male Aurora Bluetail Damselfly
Ischnura aurora

As though he bathed - in Algae -
a tideline in his eyes -
green - below Meniscus -
black above. His Gaze

gleams out of the Shadows -
his Tail - touches Light -
he swivels - like an Alidade -
degrees - tilt down - to Nought -

his thorax is - Obsidian -
his abdomen - of Rust -
I blink a Moment - look again -
and find that he is - Lost -

Dragonfly and Spider

I found a Dragonfly entangled
in a Knot of Grass -
another flew - and tended her
her wings lashed out - and Burst.

I stooped to see if Spider - lurked
her Fate already - done -
when she launched - into my face -
recoiled - and was gone -

Swamp Harrier
Circus approximans

I see you - old ring-tail
harrying the Height -
lifting your Pinions
losing your Weight -

ragged your flying
lifting - through haze
black-tipped your Primaries -
sulphured - your gaze -

legs hanging - ready -
talons held loose -
pale iris - narrowing -
hovering - close -

Two more Swamp Harriers are airborne, quartering the open water – hefting through the wind on straggled wings. The water's edge is a scum of discarded feathers – the air is tasselled with Flies. When I approach, the shallow water turns into a turmoil of tiny Fishes who propel themselves in one body toward the deep. I turn back to a sandy trail that undulates through Peppermints – hoping to circle the southernmost of the lakes – but the water is increasingly distant through the trees' thin trunks. It ends in an intensity of leaves and Cicadas tending to a hollow where Snakes might go to cool themselves, or catch perhaps a Frog. I lose my glasses – find them again – retrace my steps. I hear a crashing of Kangaroos but do not see them.

Back out near the open water, the goats are making progress through the brambles. Most of the leaves are eaten, the bine stems trampled. The goats are looking hot and bored. I might be the highlight of their day. They pause to gaze, then keep on eating. Beyond them I hear a solitary boom – perhaps a Bittern …

11 December 2023

*Northwest Wetland (Browns Road entrance)
to the north shore of Maringup Creek
6.26 p.m. to 7.53 p.m.*

The sun turns yellow ochre - then honeyed -
haloing a herd of Kangaroos and Joeys -
bathing the Paperbarks' western edges
in sinking light. One branch creaks
against another. A Swamphen's wheezing scream
reverberates through Reedmace - the Damselflies
already sleeping. I walk down Browns Road
led by a Fantail who loops in air from reed
to reed - and as the flat land opens out
the songs of Warblers splash and resound.

I round a corner into the wetland - to the creak
of Grasshoppers - and the Warbler now
is louder - a brash clatter of dashing notes -
a cascade of shattered crystal - and behind it -
softer - the tentative whisper of a Grassbird.
Shelducks fly over in a gabble and flurry -
something scuttles through the water. Wind stirs
the reed leaves - so the sun is filtered differently
every moment. I withdraw - awed - continue
down the pathway - to a second opening
in the Yandjet - where last time a Harrier
was perched upon the *Banksia*. Her branch
is empty now - but still fringed with fluff

of Yandjet seeds - and the sun sinks
directly behind it - lighting their filaments.

Faster than expected - it is gone behind a dune -
so I hurry on to find the open water - too rushed
to stop for insects. I want to catch the sunlight waning
over the broad spillage of Maringup Creek.

I am there in time to see Black Ducks flying
fast-winged - eastward for their roosts -
and in one nook between the reeds - a Swan
turns her crimson face toward me
and floats slowly - resisting flight.
Ibises fly in skeins - black against the Golden -
toward a lone tree tall above the marshes.
The wind buffets. I follow a petering path
deep into the Bracken - watching every footfall
for Snakes. Wrens pivot and raise alarm calls
and through the Peppermints' dark trunks
I glimpse two Swamp Harriers quartering
the open water - starkly screeching - hungry.

Still - all around - there is Reed Warbler song -
as if the same bird had followed all the way -
and the resonant plopping dewdrop calling
of the Musk Duck hidden away in the impenetrable
thatch of wind-caught stems and ribboned leaves.

I wander back - and as the light intensifies
and reddens - clinging to the horizon -

the Warblers' songs are ever louder.
Last Dragonflies are homing on their roosts -
first evening Moths are warming up their wings.

I am back among the Paperbarks -
the path in total darkness - birdsong
a crescendo amid the boles. I turn
toward the road - light my torch
in time to see a tiny exquisite Dugite
perfect in its curves - twisting away
unruffled - dissolving into grass.

12 December 2023
At home

Exhaustion is a lot like walking through long grass which is not your home at all, but the home of Snakes – except that when I'm at Eungedup, there's a purpose to all the tension. Chronic fatigue bites you anyway, no matter how carefully you tread, and it has venom which produces an endless variety of neurotoxic symptoms. On the one hand, there are cognitive symptoms, like an inexorable weighting toward inattention – which is in direct proportion to the importance of the subject being discussed – and forgetfulness, which can happen in a matter of a second. Then there's a compelling weakness, which flows in unannounced, like a tidal wave, and can transform you within minutes from a human being driven by purpose and inspiration into a flaccid, directionless nonentity. There are symptoms which you feel physically, but are invisible to others, like the strange prickling in the extremities, which comes upon you when you've really pushed the boundaries of exertion, as I used to do every day at school, and now do when I'm visiting Eungedup. You are lying down to sleep, knowing how you need it, and the prickling comes to keep you wide awake. When you get up the next day, your lower legs ache so much it causes you to stumble.

Very few of the symptoms, unfortunately, are external. If they were, we sufferers of CFS would elicit pity and consideration everywhere we went. We'd carry special stickers on our windscreens, and every public building would have a built-in turret, just for climbing-up and sleeping. But there is one physical symptom that functions, in my mind, as a signal that I have definitely been pushing things too far, and I fancy others can detect it – although, now that I come to think, no one has ever commented on it.

The Nerve which makes the Eyelid twitch
and yearn for shrouding Night
connects discretely with the tongue
that whispers grimly - Nought -

and Longing finds its Lodge in me -
a Flutter and a Breath -
a yawning to engulf the Dark -
devour the whole - of Death.

Slice me open - you'll not find -
beneath the Mask of Face
a clue to what provoked the Twitch
or motive for the Force -

but only Tissue - bare-exposed -
no Tick that caused the Itch -
and then it will be vain to grieve -
twice as vain - to stitch -

I am certain there are nervous tics which would be noticeable to a dispassionate observer when I am negotiating the grassy footpath that circles the weedy area between the wetlands of Eungedup – one of the two places on the site where I regularly see Snakes when it is warm enough. But it's easier than negotiating life, partly because the required concentration is of limited duration, partly also because I know for certain that any Snake I nearly tread on is twice as afraid of me as I am of it, and mostly because when I'm at Eungedup, I'm always driven by some inspirational obsession. If I can only stand long enough in such and such a place, I'm bound to see a Bittern. If I set my voice recorder out there long enough and my batteries are charged, I'm sure to catch a Crake call. If I'm there enough at nightfall, I'll learn where the Harriers go to roost, or get to watch a Rakali slipping into water.

And this time, as far as fear of Snakes is concerned, I've hit upon the ultimate solution. If I go and seek them out deliberately, I'll never step on them inadvertently, because I'll always be looking out for them, as top priority and fount of inspiration. Oh yes – I've scotched the Snake without killing it, and I'm pleased.

If only I could do that with chronic fatigue. I'll keep the hypnagogic hallucinations – those I rather enjoy. You goddamn inexorable lassitude and twitching eyelid – I'm looking out for you most keenly – and this time I won't step on you, at all.

14 December 2023

At home

I have been writing a rave review of a new book by an English poet, Phil Barnett, called *Birds Knit My Ribs Together*. The title was what caused me to ask if I could have a review copy, so that I could read it before it was published – but I am taken aback to discover when I receive it that Phil has also suffered from chronic fatigue, so badly that at one point he was completely unable to walk. In its incandescently beautiful fifty pages, his book speaks eloquently about what it is to lose mobility, and its words are haunted by birds, flitting in and out of the beauty and the pain.

More astonishing still, he has also written a poem – very different in style from my own – inspired by a moment when he too came face-to-face with a flying dragonfly. And when he writes that birds knit his ribs together, he really means it. The natural world is a part of his healing process, certainly, but it is much more than that. He has reached the point where he feels himself to be a part of the "ebb" and "flow". He is blending in, and the world around him is making a different kind of sense. I read the poems repeatedly, with something like a rising sense of triumph.

I am also re-reading *Hen Harrier Poems*, a book about our Swamp Harrier's European counterpart, by Colin Simms. He has decided that "information is carried best by poetry, verse" – information about the birds and their habitats, that is, because Simms actively avoids the centre of attention. John Clare discovered the same thing before him, in his poems about the nests of birds and Harvest Mice. The Northamptonshire "peasant poet" – turned, apparently, "madman" – speaks most eloquently of self when he is contemplating a tightly woven ball of grass, out of which a mother Harvest Mouse emerges, dragging her babies at her teats. J.A. Baker, too, in his tour de force, *The Peregrine*, never tells us anything about himself – just determinedly, obsessively observes the birds. He obliterates himself, yet re-emerges fully made, and although his masterpiece has the visual look of prose, it is certainly pure poetry he has written.

Poetry is not "therapy", or a way of holding onto self, as it is often marketed as being; it is an end in itself. But when we write poems that grow out of direct, specific experience of nature – in other words, out of unsolicited encounters with completely other and unexpected beings – they can become the spell we weave that dissolves our sense of self and sets us free from its constraints. We lose our selves in place, and find ourselves dissolved and re-formed, like the utterly liquidated caterpillar which is reconstituting its being inside the chrysalis. It's something that artificial intelligence, having neither self, experience, nor the desire for dissolution of the self into something bigger, will never be able to achieve.

Writing in poetry forces us to condense – it pushes us to the heart of the matter. It resonates, too, with the rhythms of walking. I find this especially with a Dickinsonian style of ballad metre. The lyrics come to me while I'm in the act of walking, and I rush to put them onto paper, or speak them into a voice recorder. Recently, a poem came to me whilst I was filming the track which runs through the Peppermint woodland between the Eungedup wetlands, so I spoke it as I walked, with the video still recording. Kangaroos burst across the trail in front of me – I paused and kept on talking.

It makes me think that perhaps Emily Dickinson almost trod on a Snake while she was out walking, and as she continued on her way 'A narrow fellow in the grass' was forming in her mind. She had to hurry home to write it down, and that last line, about feeling "Zero at the Bone", must surely have been bursting from her, as if the chrysalis had split.

14 December 2023
*Northwest Wetland (Browns Road entrance)
to the north shore of Maringup Creek
3.06 p.m. to 5.19 p.m.*

A Tiger Snake hunting is almost languorous -
coils gliding between the swamp-lush blades of grass -
sticking her deadly beauteous head into holes
prospecting for Frogs - slowly retracting it again
unsuccessful - resting motionless awhile in sun
to let it warm her glaze of scales - pushing in deeper
where the grass grows lanker - diffidently withdrawing -
pausing again to become a lithe unending glyph
of gleaming - then on a whim deciding to wend away

                                  and disappearing.

Swamp Harriers hunting are only languid
when they're soaring - and high above them
a Whistling Kite - almost vanishing into altitude -
but at some signal the Harriers swoop downward -
I grab my binoculars to track one scudding
just above the water - flashing in and out of vision
through gaps in the Yandjet - so wildly close
I see the midribs of his feathers - glimpse his cold
yellow Moorhen's nightmare of an eye - and then
he's circling up - to Elevation - not a single wingbeat -
turning languid on the wind - meeting his mate in midair

                                    disappearing.

A lone Western Rosella flies - chattering in terror
straight over me - pursued half-heartedly by
a Brown Goshawk with a scalloped breast - who turns
in air to eye me - the lust for killing dying in her eye

                        and disappearing.

A Grasshopper flips in front of me - living essence
of a grass leaf - perching on a grass stem - aligning
her eyes with heaven - concentrating her long face into
a leaf-tip

                            disappearing -

I turn to see a second Tiger Snake - hunting languid
right behind me. She hunts a long and lissom while
then finds the Yandjet shadows -

                            disappearing.

I hear a Frog screech in the reeds - imagine his writhing -
slack back limbs relaxing - into languor -
his world of Moths - and Flies - and Beetles -

                            disappearing -

Wood Sandpipers
Tringa glareola

Sandpipers - dapper Waders
up to their breasts in water
heads submerged in sunlit wetland
a Globe away - from Arctic winter -

raise their bills - pip staccato -
when they glimpse me - through the stems -
I fade - backwards - loth to flush
such weatherers of winds - and storms -

born of Tundra - shaped for gales -
seeking shades - and wooded lakes -
at home - alike - with Arctic Foxes
and with swamps alive - with Snakes.

Grasshoppers
Austroicetes cruciata?

For Grasshoppers - I've barely waited
though they scatter - every step -
some like withered - fallen gumleaves
some like broken twigs - that leap -

until one drops - upon my finger
freckled as - my freckled skin -
freckles in the wings - and eye-globes
as if - encrypted - by Design -

Common Grass Blue Butterfly
Zizina labradus

One perches on a leaf - of Clover
one grips a stem - of flowering Grass
lit by Sun beneath its anthers -
ringed antennae - gently pulse -

joined end-to-end - hindwings furry -
bridging bodies - in the Lush -
suspended over muds - where fishes
writhe through grass-leaves half-awash.

17 December 2023
South side of Maringup Creek (Manoni Road entrance)
6.44 p.m. to 8.00 p.m.

I've only started part way down the path
when a Sacred Kingfisher curves in air across
from left to right - trailing in her scissor bill
a long limp Legless Lizard - or perhaps
a new-hatched Snake - and chooses a higher branch
to gulp it down. On the grass before the reeds
two Meelyas are grazing - but out across the water
Straw-Necked Ibises are already at their roosts -
bare branches of dead trees amid the reeds
bearing them like heavy fruit already overripe.

Motorbike Frogs start in chorus and stop again.
Ravens speak and answer in the Peppermints
behind me - and somewhere in the distant raft
of leaves and stems - the harsh churr of a Crake
is stirring. A Brown Goshawk whirls over
on rapid wingbeats - Tree Martins spiral higher.
Kookaburras scuttle - young ones chuntering -
Wood Ducks hiss and hustle. A Grassbird
tests the atmosphere with gentle whistles.
One Kookaburra flies to ground - stabbing something
in the grass. A Swamphen bursts her explosive
bubble. Two Swans are floating silhouettes - one
upends - then rights herself - glides - dips the dark
question of her neck downwards again. White Ibises
fly straight over open water - a flock of seventy.

Pelicans grunt and stumble - invisible behind the reeds.
A Musk Duck cocks his fan-tail upward - fills
his throat and slaps the water with his feathers - while
a Shoveler - bill like something melted - leaves
a straight and gleaming wake along the darker water.

By now the sun has sunk and everywhere
Mosquitoes seek and needle. A gap in cloud
reveals a crescent moon - and somewhere
on the grass a Frog cries out in pain - protracted -
and sounds of wings and webbed feet on the water
mingle with the sloppy bonks of Banjo Frogs.
Far across the wetland - a late Warbler strikes up
as Mosquitoes gather in a high-pitched cloud
above my head - and zero in on fingers exposed
as I am writing - this. I stay as long as I can stand -
then beat a tactical retreat - as Slender Tree Frogs
swell their throats amid the Peppermints - pausing
only to lap up Mosquitoes - weaving with the Banjos
and the Motorbikes their crisp bright folksong in the dark.

20 December 2023
At home

Another crushing lull. I stare at the ceiling and cling to fleeting memories of the closing wings of Butterflies – the shimmers on wings of Dragonflies.

I throw my Inspiration - out -
it falls - to a Black Hole -
the Word can only whirl about
Extinguishment - of Soul -

the circuit of my World - is flung
into hungry Dark -
with all the Beauty - all the Art -
every human Work -

yet in the very Vortex - look -
it flies - on fragile Wings -
the Fragment indestructible
enduring all our Wrongs -

airborne Tissue - veined for strength -
alive - and ever sought -
elusive - tangible - untamed -
through the Blast - of Nought -

26 December 2023

*Northwest Wetland (Browns Road entrance)
to the north shore of Maringup Creek
7.52 a.m. to 10.40 a.m.*

The Reed Warblers are almost silent -
so now I notice the quiet whicker of wings
from Black Ducks coming swiftly - a Spoonbill
flying solitary - tree-height in a circle -
a Swamphen's wheeze - a distant rizzle
of Cicadas woven with the needling songs
of wrens. Light raindrops ruffle the surface.

All the way to Maringup Creek I see no Snakes -
and now overlooking open water I still myself
so the Birds who fled webfooted at my coming
slowly return - paddling out and dabbling.
I step sideways to change my view between
the Yandjet - half-expecting Bitterns - but
I only hear a pair of Ravens tracing a sickle
high over Maringup Creek. A few Tree Frogs
awake - not enough to stop me calling this
a silence. A female Wren perches half-way
up a stem - one foot up - one foot down.
A Cormorant flies over. Wind stirs a little.
Wattlebirds fly above the rushes - swooping off
through Peppermints. Dragonflies begin to wake.

With halting gait a Spotted Crake is by the water
stepping cautiously - bending to the mud.

She senses me - turns and scuttles so fast
I might have dreamt her. But now she's back -
tail pointing to the zenith a second - body hinging
downward - testing - tasting - gone again
in a blinking.

    A Swan announces her arrival
with white-pinioned wing-claps on the water -
heavy body and neck of ebony stretched
a webbed foot's width above the surface.
The Crake appears - disappears - reappears
as a Cormorant settles on distant water and
another takes to wing - twisting a loop - then
flying straight - receding. The Swan herds
her Cygnets - fully grown - ahead of her -
they batter the water with eager wings -
touching surface beyond a screen of reeds.
The Spotted Crake departs - stays gone -
and I walk on.

    Pale-capped Mushrooms stud
the shorter grass among arable weeds -
rusty-seeded Docks - greyish hairy Willowherbs -
Scarlet Pimpernels - Centauries and Thistles -
a Native Bee - amber-bellied - feeds off yellow
flowers of weeds. A brown Wasp is hauling
an inert larva over sand. A Blue Skimmer perches
on a yellow Vetch.

There in that weediest place
between the wetlands I find him - Tiger Snake
long as my arm-span - emerging unassuming
around a Dock plant - body barred with embers -
hunting among the Pimpernels with a magnificent
silk-smooth head that gleams in sunlight - languid
as before - wending his way through thistledown
which sometimes catches in the glisten of his scales -
then suddenly stabbing downward into turf -
pulling back his cocked head and swallowing.
I see pink gums inside his open jaw and the flailing leg
of the Gumleaf Grasshopper he's consuming -
his wide mouth wet and flexible. He probes further -
stabs again - lifts his head - devouring - then
progressively vanishes into a low clump of Willowherb -
his tail still disappearing as his sleek head and
obsidian eyes re-emerge - much closer to me.

                                                I retreat -
and find myself on the edge of open water
where a dark and downy Crake chick picks
her way on spindly legs upon the silt - pecking
at Duckweed - flicking her tail skyward like
her parents. She's intent on her catching
all the long minutes I spend slowly approaching.

Spotted Crake Chick
Porzana fluminea

Splay-footed Crake chick
slightly grey about the face -
black upon the crest and ears
beady-eyed Duckweed taster -
tester of everything that may
be tasty - steps deliberately
on elongated toes - flicks
her tiny tail-tip - staggers
at a Dragonfly - takes fright
and shoots aside - instantly
re-emerges - runs in spurts -
bites Crustaceans with beaky
tweezers - flashes the tiny
white splash of her bottom -
has a drink - takes a dibble -
darts into a shady dapple -

and instantly the frantic cackle of her parent
ratchets in the Reedmace - I imagine her
huddled to the speckled breast - safe from
Danger - safe from Harrier - safe -

                                        from Tiger Snake.

Far off - visible only in binoculars -
a Swamp Harrier rips at something underfoot
on a muddy edge of water. A Musk Duck

glides alarmingly close - seemingly unconcerned -
and the Harrier raises imperious wings -
lifts off - flash of white at base of tail -
vanishes beyond reeds. Around the Musk Duck
extends a lazily expanding wake.

29 December 2023
At home

My skin prickles. It kept me awake last night. The night before, it was a single, whining, elusive Mosquito. I batter furiously at my mind. I distract myself with internet videos of Rakalis and Bitterns. It's midday, but I lie back down in bed.

Biological detritus -
is all I really am -
I'm waiting for - dispersal -
and trying to be - calm -

I labour in - the Struggle -
I brace against - the Blast -
I cower - in admission
that I am only - Dust -

yet rail against Injustice -
yet chafe against Decline
yet rage - against Extinction -
although I leave - alone -

expiring - in - admitting -
that Dust is - Everything -

1 January 2024

*Northwest Wetland (Browns Road entrance)
to the north shore of Maringup Creek
5.29 p.m. to 8.26 p.m.*

Along Browns Road the Reed Warbler's song
is the weft for every other sound - the weave
is the reedy calls of Shelducks answered
by Ravens' voices - the hurried startled whirr
of a Black Duck's wings - the eternal stir
of the wind itself - animating the fabric of reeds
on the taut loom of a windswept darkening evening.

A few paces further - and everything is stiller -
the reeds scarcely astir - only hidden Wrens
are singing amid Grasshoppers' crisp stridulations.

I make my way to the weedy field
where last time Snakes were hunting.
The pointed Mushrooms' caps have flattened,
wearing spores like smuts - some are chewed
or broken at the stems. Spoonbills fly
straight-necked above me and a Cormorant
takes a hairpin bend the length and breadth
of Maringup. Beyond the weeds the track
turns sandy - a Kangaroo pauses on his haunches -
turns to take me in - bounds at my approach -
and I look down to see the sand is cobbled
in a wide swathe of pointing sigils -
the long-toed footmarks of a herd of Roos.

The sun has set. Rain is coming. This evening
on that muddy reed-edge where last time I saw
a Harrier strip her prey - two Shelducks
are preening - and further off in open water
on a tiny silted island - a second pair have settled.

Australian Pelican
Pelecanus conspicillatus

Ungainly on the land
a Pelican in flight
scarcely stirs a wing at all -
like a quill afloat

on thermals over Maringup -
wing feathers spilling air -
makes a stately - proud descent
levelling out - afar -

meeting with the water-glaze
with hardly wave or wake -
weightlessness her mystery -
effortless - her work.

Yellow-Billed Spoonbill
Platalea flavipes

A Spoonbill's heading in to roost -
his butter-textured bill

held out flat - and at a stretch
unswerving in the squall -

it might seem an impediment -
a load to keep out front -
for dabbling - and filtering -
no finer implement -

I've seen them knee-deep in the shallows
feeding - in a swerve -
more attuned to taste and touch
than anything - alive -

I want to see across the open water
so I climb a spreading Peppermint - wedging
myself between two boles - feet at head-height -
and spy an Ibis roost on thin dead trees
that stand in water - branches bleached
as skeletons. A Harrier flies as if intent
on landing in my Tree - sees me - glares down
with predator eyes - rears in air - and soars away.
Kookaburras ratchet up into laughter.
Lower down at reed-height - Crakes
join the cacophony - and still it's there -
texturing everything - getting louder
in the spreading dusk - straw-coloured
Reed Warbler spilling out his multicoloured soul.

Wind drives in and shakes the Peppermint
around me - an arc of waves approaches

over water. Then comes rain - a wide
and shifting curtain - drenching the bark grain
where I cling - stippling the surface of the water.

I climb down - switch on my head-torch -
make my way back through darkling woodland
toward Browns Road - hear the weighty thumps
of Kangaroos and scurries of mammals in Bracken.
The track's become alive with Motorbike Frogs
of every size - some fat and mottled brown -
some spindly - entirely green. They ogle blearily
in torchlight - leap aside or sit tight awaiting
Mosquitoes. I hear one on the track ahead
cry aloud in agony - and half-expect to see it
gobbled by a Snake - but find instead a small Frog
desperately flailing half-way down the gullet
of a larger. At my approach they spring apart
like charged particles - the bright green victim
seemingly undamaged - the fat brown aggressor
frantic - indignant - ricocheting in retreat.
The trackway heaves with Frogs - the air
a haze of whining Mozzies.

      Driving away
down Lake Saide Road takes twice as long -
slowing down to swerve around
Frogs and yet more
      Frogs.

4 January 2024
At home

I lie down on my back searching film I've taken
for a Bittern I might have missed - enlarging it
section by section. One might be skygazing
in the middle of any frame - but what should be
the slant of an upraised Bittern bill - is only
a reed that's hanging broken - a darker shade is just
a shadow in the gaps among the deeper reeds -
that stray enticing movement merely caused
by currents and cross-currents in the wind.

Pinned to my bed - it's becoming an obsession
because with Bitterns you can be staring straight
at one - and seeing only gaps and reeds.

Sometimes searching for a Bittern that may
or may not be hidden is like searching for the link

                                              in me that's missing.

6 January 2024

At home

I have discovered some drone footage, taken a year ago, which systematically covers the whole extent of Eungedup. When on foot, especially when the water is high, there are only a few places where I can get a full view of open water. Most of the wetlands are hemmed in by reeds – a source of frustration when I am trying to glimpse Waders and Waterbirds and search for Rakalis, but of course, also a significant advantage to the wild things themselves. Eungedup does not exist for the benefit of human beings, but for itself and for its inhabitants, and the beds of Yandjet, which come right up to the edges of the paths in most places, provide the privacy of true wilderness.

The video is fourteen minutes long. I stare at it agog. The drone flies out over the wetland to the west of Browns Road. There is a quaggy footpath, itself lined and overhung with reeds, that runs out into the middle of this area, where a dilapidated old farm shed stands, open to the elements. Sometimes, this path is just about walkable, but this summer, the grass on it has grown long and bright green, and it is alive with hunting Tiger Snakes. But with the drone footage, I can see what is hidden to me on the ground, and draw a more detailed and accurate representation of the positions of the reedbeds and open water on the map I have been creating. As the drone swoops around the edges of the open water, I see flocks of birds – some floating on the surface, some flying just above it. Most of them are unidentifiable at this height, but the Swans stand out with their dark, hooked necks. For a moment, a Welcome Swallow flits past, very close to the camera.

Now the drone swoops back toward Browns Road, and crosses it, heading out over Lake Saide to its east. Lake Saide is totally surrounded by impenetrable reeds on all sides, so it has been a tantalising mystery to me. A while ago, I climbed up the arching trunk of a tree on the edge of the track, just so that I could get a glimpse of the lake, but all I saw was a flash of sunlit water, distant among the reed tops. The drone reveals a broad expanse of deep open water clear of vegetation, which I had assumed until now was mostly choked by reeds. The drone hovers over a part of the surrounding Peppermint woodland, through which a small creek, Scotsdale Brook, runs out of the lake.

Soon we are soaring back across Lake Saide, and heading directly south along Browns Road, across the weedy square of dry land where the *Banksia*s grow, and where friendly goats were eradicating the blackberries last month, and we're up above Maringup Creek. For a minute, I can see the Manoni Road entrance, and the low, grassy hill where I have stood a couple of times at sunset, overlooking the wetland and being bitten by Mosquitoes. The taller trees to the west, and the dead trees in the middle of the water, where I have seen Ibises and Spoonbills flying to roost, stand out clearly as the drone rotates. We're flying out to the far westernmost extent of Maringup, and the drone swivels northward, looking out over the sandy tracks, worn more by Kangaroos than by human beings, through the Peppermint woodland that divides the bodies of water. This is the place where I have been whiling away the hours chasing Dragonflies and Sun Moths.

At last, the drone is heading back toward Browns Road – back to the place where most of my pilgrimages have started. My bones are aching and periodically a swooning sensation comes over me. I would not have been able to make it out to Eungedup today, but with the help of the footage, I can be there, augmenting what I know with a new and detailed perspective on the place.

I watch the video again and again, sometimes pausing it, and dragging it along frame by frame. In my imagination, I'm not on a virtual ride on a drone's back any more. I'm a Swamp Harrier, reconnoitering my territory. Those flocks of smaller birds, flying with their wingtips just above the water's surface, are the source of my next meal. One of those trees is my roost – others are excellent vantage points for when I need a daytime rest. There is the gnarled *Banksia* which crooks its arm so that I can perch in view of reeds and open water. I rise up sunward, bank and soar – and hover for a long forever.

7 January 2024

*Northwest Wetland (Browns Road entrance)
to the north shore of Maringup Creek
4.30 a.m. to 7.05 a.m.*

The stars are fading into light - and already
the wetland's wide awake. Along Browns Road
the places where I pause - the gaps in reeds -
are side-chapels tapestried in green all down
the long nave of the trail - and each is jewelled
with birdsong. They beckon me a moment -
but I must rush to watch the rising sun.

Beyond Maringup - clouds are coloured rose
and Pelicans and Cormorants take wing.
Spotted Crakes rush headlong into reeds -
re-emerge a moment - and retreat - but one
has dropped a gift upon the silt - a dark grey
contour feather - white-banded - only here
at all because it's windless. I stoop to pick it up
and here are footprints - fresh as morning -
pointing out to open water - one forepaw
and a back foot slightly webbed - claw marks
pressing deep into the mud: Rakali. He's left
at faintest first light to seek his prey of Fishes -
or if he's hungry - Frogs. I've missed him
this time - but now I know his hideout's
somewhere near. I gaze on open water until
reflections and the real can't be distinguished
in the glaze - and Frogs begin their throbbing.

Behind me I hear thuds and frenzied leaping -
Kangaroos departing through the scrub -
and when I move - Coots and Ducks skedaddle -
wings wildly flapping - flat feet slapping
madly at the surface. Their clatter lingers
long behind them in the threshed and hectic
silvers of their wakes. An Australasian Grebe -
it seems - ignores me - flashing cheeks of yellow
every time she turns - bending neck of chestnut -
paddling further out - then diving - and when
my held breath is bursting - bobbing up. If only
all birds could ignore me like this Grebe.

I climb up in my Tree to see the sun appearing
and slowly all the Waterbirds return - floating
out from Yandjet - flying in and braking -
making flurries of white water. A Black Duck
upends and rights himself - I watch the drip
of water gather on his bill-tip - well - and fall -
a late Pied Cormorant seems to be still roosting
on an overhanging branch above the shore.

I hurry back toward those reedy chapels -
now the birdsong's voluble - intense -
and in the first I wait - and still each muscle.
My veil of anonymity - descends.

Reed Warbler
Acrocephalus australis

I stand to watch a Spotted Crake
and realise - I am watched -
a flitting bird has caught my glimpse
where that Yandjet - twitched.

Now he's flitted back again -
a dark stripe through his eye -
I stare - he stares - he grips a reed -
disdains - to fly away.

He flicks about - from reed - to reed -
swoops up - to catch a Fly -
he's been hunting since first light -
now he can sing - all day.

A Warbler's filled my cup with joy
so full it slops - to spill -
a blessing gained - by nothing more
than simply standing - still -

I move on to the second reedy chapel - freeze again -
and straight away a Spotted Crake emerges -
points her tail to sky - her bill to ground - commences
pecking systematically at mud. She moves across
the only open patch amid the reeds - traversing
this and that way - and as I'm breathless watching -
out steps a tall Buff-Banded Rail in finest plumage -

and I realise how small the Crake was as she's fleeing.
But then the Rail is gone again - and she's creeping
out to finish off where she began - but at her side
another bird's emerging - breast of greyest slate -
back of dark mahogany - and a bright red staring eye -
a Spotted and a Spotless Crake together. Then
two Shelducks - launching with a clatter -
sound alarms in sky - and all are gone.

Spotless Crake
Zapornia tabuensis

Shadow bird - without a star -
tentative - of gait -
opposite - of Spotted Crake -
bird the light - forgot -

wings of dark mahogany -
breasted - as with slate -
eye like Mars - on clouded night
and fiendish hard - to spot -

stalking by - a Spotted Crake -
noirish - with a plot -
to doubly prove - Eungedup
is not a Crakeless - spot.

Skeletons

I've stumbled on skeletons here in the woods
with long bones as big as my own -
and skulls quite as heavy - lime on the earth
mossy and half-overgrown -

these were of Kangaroos - fallen like trees
left here to rot - and forgotten -
and nobody wandered - this far in these woods -
to mourn - or to smell something rotten -

and here is a skeleton - light as the feathers
still clinging - today - to the wings.
Pelican? Or Ibis? The wing-tips are black -
and gone are your yawpings - for songs.

I could turn you over - dig for the skull -
diagnose - by the shape of your bill -
Pelican? Or Ibis? But you break - at my touch -
and I'm too hemmed - by Bracken - to tell -

☙

I had been hoping all this time that I could gather the strength to come to Eungedup at first light – now I have done it. I drive away still under the enchantment of the Reed Warbler and the Crakes, and effusive about the Rakali's footprints, which had been exactly where, over the past several days, I had been planning to look for them. At the T-junction, I turn left instead of right, just on a whim, and find myself on a newly tarmacked road. Kangaroos are everywhere, and the road – and my car – are clearly still new concepts to which they are adjusting. Adults and Joeys hop along the roadside, keeping pace with me, suddenly darting under spaces they have made beneath the fences.

On my right, another wetland opens out – not part of Eungedup itself, but with similar fauna and flora, and wide open to the roadside. I stop the car, get out and scan the reeds with my binoculars, hoping against hope for a Bittern. More Coots skitter madly across the surface of the lake, tilting their white heads toward the risen sun.

I drive a little further, and come at last upon a dead end, and a heavily padlocked gate. "GREAT SOUTHERN LIME MINE SITE" says the sign in great black letters which remind me of the first chapter of *Watership Down*, virtually my Bible when I was a child – and underneath it in blood-red: "TRESPASSERS WILL BE PROSECUTED". This is why the road, which is still just an area of wilderness on Google Maps, has been flailed through here and tarmacked: to serve the mine that steals the lime of Nullaki. The road winds all the way around Eungedup's northern and western quarters, and I drive back reflecting on the obvious fact that our precious wetland was purchased for posterity not a moment too soon.

I am slipping my vehicle into four-wheel drive and wending my way around unmapped lanes, when suddenly I come upon a gaggle of Guinea Fowl, skittering apparently mindlessly – although I am sure they are just discombobulated by the unexpected appearance of a car – all across the lane. There's no way I can swerve around them: they have a kamikaze look about them which tells me that they would just walk straight underneath my wheels, and there is a bluegrass song playing on my stereo which matches their – and my – mood of incredulity. So, I just stop the car, think about turning off the ignition, and wait until the Guinea Fowl decide for themselves what they should do. Slowly, their delightful minds perhaps slightly deadened by domestication, they gobble and gabble and wander haphazardly off the road. I'm suppressing laughter as the bluegrass banjos on.

It's only as I'm shifting into gear and moving off, the road mercifully clear, that I realise precisely what it is that's so amusing: these domestic birds, with their speckled plumage and jerky, sudden movements, are overfed equivalents of the elusive Spotted Crake. If one had – by some miracle – flown over Eungedup and dropped a feather, I might easily have been fooled.

9 January 2024

*Northwest Wetland (Browns Road entrance)
to the north shore of Maringup Creek, and on the road beside
where Scotsdale Brook runs out of Lake Saide
4.08 a.m. to 6.30 a.m.*

Along the footpath on the way to Maringup -
I count sixty-one Motorbike Frogs. Some leap
in leggy frenzy as I pass them by - most seem tired
from a long night's lapping up of Moths - these
sit tight - gaze at me blearily in the torchlight.

There's the vaguest haze of red beyond Maringup
and a Black Duck quacks laughter in the darkness.
The Motorbike Frogs out in the water are hoarse
and throaty - Slender Tree Frogs chip in higher pitched -
they sound like tinsel. Banjo Frogs offer occasional plonks
to the slowly reddening darkness. It begins to rain -
heavy drops which stipple all the water - the Frogs
quieten - and at a gap in cloud the sky begins
to lighten to a bluish silver. The clouds close up
again - the Frogs turn on full throttle - and the sky
and surface of the water are ultramarine and salmon.
Reeds are curtains - draped in deepest shadow.
The rain falters - drizzles - slows - stops completely.
A first Cicada strikes up - and then a sudden - dense
and high-pitched drone - Mosquitoes rising
in massive clouds - and a Swamphen sneezing.
A smatter of birdsong starts fitfully - then rises
to a chorus - Red-Winged and Splendid Fairywrens

cause everything to shimmer. Grasshoppers chitter
in longer grass. I wade a little way into the water
sending steel-blue ripples through reflections
of reddened clouds. I walk to find my climbing-Tree -
seat myself in the lower branches - and watch
the day broadening and wakening all Eungedup.

A white feather
                falls
                          from a great height -
        perhaps an Egret's
                          breast feather
              or a White Ibis's -
        right into the water
                          in the middle of Maringup.

I do not see its owner -
                just the feather
                          dithering in windlessness
      unhurried
             in descent.

In my binoculars I see it
                      kiss the water.

Crake calls crack up the distance.
        Calls of five Cockatoos
                are aching echoes
                        over where the feather
                                    fell.

A Cormorant flies
    with purpose -
        has a change of heart
and turns
    flying back - hurriedly -
        the way it came.

Black Ducks announce their arrivals
    around a corner of Maringup
        with wide-spreading wakes
            and raucous quacks
        announcing the end of night
as daylight chases rose-colours
        from the water.

A Shoveler's spreading wake
        breaks into
    one long straight line running from his left side -
            on his
            right side
            ripples
            doppler
            outwards
            in an arc -
                his bill drips silver
        distilling
            all the essence
                of the freshly
breaking Day.

Red-Winged and Splendid Fairywrens
Malurus spp.

Elegans and *splendens* - glimpses of lapis
agleam in the green - weaving your songs -
like jewelled threads through reeds -
ever present texture. Swamps and billabongs

are stitched with your glistenings - flitting from trees
into the wetland - trinkets with eyes
that gleam into dreaming - bijou delights
under brightening skies -
condensing the daylight to bodies the size
of flowers of iris - or large butterflies -
flying out over waters - clutching to stems -
singing the sunlight - embodying - gleams -

Inland Thornbill
Acanthiza apicalis

Amid the reeds - I'm standing -
their knops above my head -
and up above the straps of leaves
Spoonbills fly - abroad -

leaves that hem about a World
for the scuttling Crake -
I wait in here - screened from sight
and watch the Birds - awake -

and hear the smattering of song
that shimmers all about -
when here - flies a pert-tailed bird
swift as passing thought -

and emits a scolding song
of molten notes - and chips -
he swivels on his spike of reed -
scolds again - then drops

out of sight - in shadows
where I can never catch
another glimpse of him - yet he
can still - securely - watch.

Where the Crakes Hunt

I marvel how this little patch
of rich and deep-brown mud
sustains a varied tribe - of Birds
whose eyes are blazing red -

who search it so consistently
there is no spot untouched
by testing bills that tweak the silt -
and no place unwatched.

A baby Swamphen stalks here too
on legs that hold him high -

so his belly's level with
a Spotless Crake's fierce eye -

and all of them subsist - on mud
or what the mud - can grow -
on islands made of rotted reeds -
surrounded by - the Flow -

Five Chestnut Teals - fore-feathers whistling in flight
curve away above me - white flashes on their wings'
leading edges. The Crakes take fright - shoot into hiding.
I walk away from the wetland into the Paperbarks
and find feathers scattered haphazard across my way -
small black primaries, secondaries, breast feathers
and what's left of the tail. Two tiny - splintered -
bloodied bones are trailed about the undergrowth
and nothing else remains. I may not have seen
a Harrier this morning - but I recognise her work -
the cold pragmatic callousness of it - the casual
expertise for killing - plucking - shearing through
                                                the bones.

I drive away up Browns Road – and on a whim, pull over where Scotsdale Brook leaves Lake Saide and passes beneath the road. A flock of Spoonbills flies up in panic, clapping their wings and grunting wildly. Seconds pass. I don't see her until she's launched herself into air with a ragged, frenzied flight – plumage a Harrier's colour – but heavier of build, bill like a long-pointed bodkin. There is mud splashed on the car window. I strain to see her clearly: her brown and paler feathers beyond the brownness of the mud-stains. Even in flight she's camouflaged. Oh – Bittern – Bittern! In midair she turns and looks at me in terror, then hefts her wings and lifts upwards over the trees – and following the Spoonbills – disappears.

I drive away, not permitting myself to feel exultant – half-failing to admit I've seen a Bittern, and feeling guilt for scaring her away. But I turn round in the road and return to where I saw her, walking out and leaning over to see where she'd been sitting. There is only bare mud and cloudy water where the Spoonbills have been wading – the flow aswirl with fishes – perfect hunting for a Bittern. Ducks swim underneath the road and chatter – a lone Spoonbill is returning to the water – but my Bittern! She is long gone and the sooner I go too, the better.

¥

There is an old Irish poem, 'An Bonnán Buí', which, in my semi-conscious state after my early mornings, has been reverberating in my mind all day. It is not at all a serious poem; its central premise is that alcohol is the elixir of life, and that if the dead Bittern, which the protagonist has just found, had only had a drop or two of something stronger than swamp water, it would still be alive. But the early part of the poem, especially in Seamus Heaney's translation of it, presents the Bittern's death as an absolute unmitigated calamity. It is not a poem that can be read in this age of extinction without those first stanzas evoking horror and remorse, because in our age, the Bitterns die not for want of any sort of drink, but because of habitat destruction and human noise.

Reports of my sighting of the Bittern are already creating a stir among those who care for Eungedup. Brad Kneebone, of the Eungedup Management Group, rings me to tell me that mine is one of only a very small handful of sightings of the local population, which has been heard much more than it has been seen. Most sightings, too, have been away from the reedbeds, where the birds are at the edges of their territories, since finding a Bittern amidst the vast swathes of Yandjet at Eungedup is probably more difficult than finding a needle in a haystack. And that makes Eungedup perfect for the Bitterns. There is no easy way for a human being to gain access to Lake Saide on foot; the Yandjet is impenetrable on all sides. That is as it should be: wilderness existing for the sake of its wild inhabitants, not for human pleasure.

But exhausted as I am, my spirits are aloft this evening because of that one, fleeting glimpse, and as I listen one more time to a recording of Seamus Heaney reading 'The Yellow Bittern', I reflect that whilst I'm not averse to a dram of malt whisky now and then, I would give all the juice of the barley in the world for the population of the Australasian Bittern in Western Australia to rise from less than a hundred, to thousands.

10 January 2024
At home

I have now admitted to myself that the "Bittern" I thought I heard in July 2022 must have been a Swamphen. Swamphens also make a booming noise, but it usually culminates in a loud sort of squeal or sneeze. I have heard this many times during my subsequent visits to Eungedup, and it has caused a creeping doubt to set in about that initial experience. If I'm right about it now, it was perhaps a forgivable misidentification driven by a desperate hope – but the bird I saw yesterday was another matter entirely: an incontrovertible living Bittern, incapable of being confused with any other bird, engraved forever in my thoughts. It lingers today in my memory as the materialisation of hope, and the way it shot up in a flurry of feathers and disappeared beyond the trees is an illustration of how fleeting and full of yearning for a better world our hope can sometimes be.

There are reasons why that sense of hope quakes on the borders of desperation. Australasian Bitterns have been dwindling alarmingly, across Australia and in New Zealand. Their habitats have been destroyed but also degraded. There are multiple records of Bitterns dying of starvation. As wetlands are destroyed, they creep out into creeks and stormwater drains, desperate for food. They burn up their own bone marrow trying to stay alive. But it is not just the destruction of wetlands which is causing this calamity – it is also the degradation of the wetlands which still exist. Eutrophication occurs when too much nitrogen flows into wetlands from surrounding farmland treated with industrial fertilisers. Massive algal blooms cloud the water so that Bitterns, who hunt exclusively by sight, cannot see into the water to hunt.

Worse still, the numbers of Bitterns are easily overestimated if they are derived from reports of booming males. Data acquired from birds which have been fitted with GPS transmitters show that a species which was previously thought to be sedentary regularly migrates between wetlands – in other words, Bitterns have been double-counted on the assumption that they are different birds when they have turned up in different locations. This discovery also shows that individual Bitterns require more than one wetland to meet their needs.

What is being achieved at Eungedup is wonderful and inspirational, but in order to flourish, Bitterns need whole chains of Eungedups, and mosaics of wild, natural habitats between them to fulfil all their dietary and breeding requirements. They need humans to be quieter: no noisy traffic or mines operating when the males are booming to attract their mates. When they walk out onto roads to hunt for sunning lizards, and then adopt their stargazing postures rather than flying away when startled by approaching cars, they need motorists who are driving slowly and attentively. And there are enough roads already – Bitterns don't need any more. A tarmacked road cleaving through the bushland right beside Eungedup is one road too many, and although it is a triumph that Eungedup itself can now no longer be directly destroyed, the agricultural practices operating in farms around it, and the lime mining activity not far away, are less easily controlled.

I have spent the morning listening to podcasts from New Zealand about scientists' efforts to learn more about Bitterns so that they can be conserved. They catch them in traps fitted with mirrors and using pre-recorded Bittern booms. The captured birds are fitted with transmitters and released, supplying much more reliable information about their habits and dispersal across the landscape. Some scientists use drones with heat-sensitive cameras to discover their positions in the wetlands. Alarmingly, one scientist developed a method, now considered antiquated and unethical, of leaning out of helicopters and dropping nets on the discombobulated birds. One researcher, Emma Williams, uses a Conservation Dog, a black Labrador, highly trained and wearing a muzzle, to track Bitterns, and especially to find birds that do not have transmitters attached already.

As I go back to bed, my strength ebbing, I am struck by the conflicting behaviours of human beings: the scientists who go to such extraordinary lengths to gather information about Bitterns so that they can be conserved, and the owners of mining companies who are prepared to dig loudly into the earth less than a kilometre away from a known nesting site and last bastion of the birds in Western Australia. The gulf in understanding mortifies me. I don't know where the miners lost their sense of wonder. And that sets me thinking about my upbringing – raised by an English teacher and a biological researcher – always surrounded by animals, camping in wildernesses, learning from an early age how to use identificatory keys, being encouraged to keep a diary and to write my own animal adventures inspired by *Watership Down*.

The apologists for mining the Nullaki Peninsula would no doubt call me a "greenie", and assume that my horror at what they are doing is confected and politically motivated. The sense of wonder that I feel, and which has been inculcated in me since childhood – not because of "environmental activism", but because of science, the arts and an abiding and sustaining relationship with the natural world – is not a part of the world of mining executives at all.

And at bottom, thinking about that yawning gulf in understanding is just so very exhausting and depleting. I know, empirically, that a bout of glandular fever – and possibly some other factors that are explainable – caused my chronic fatigue. But it sometimes feels as though my condition is just a perfectly natural response to mass extinction, and my fleeting moments of apparent wellness are like the Bittern I saw yesterday, erupting into terrified flight and disappearing beyond the trees.

Australasian Bittern
Botaurus poiciloptilus

Cryptic Bittern - living puzzle -
breath of Moonlight - hidden riddle -
conundrum on extinction's edge
lurking by - a concrete bridge -

I didn't mean to fright you - Bittern -
or interrupt your patient fishing -
I'll wait a lifetime here - to glimpse you -
muddy-mottled glyph of wishing.

I hope - Bittern - I can find you -
find - and leave you undisturbed -
to behold - but not to solve you -
ancient - noble - fleeting Bird.

Teach me - Bittern - how to tell
a world which drains and looks away
how to halt - behold you - Bittern -
so you linger - never fly.

Lend me breath of booming - Bittern -
so that I might cast a spell
of mottled umbers wet and seeping -
deliverance from concrete hell -

take me to your reedbed - Bittern -
let me sway - as reed stems do -
teach me arts of disappearing
and treading lightly - light as you -

Legend

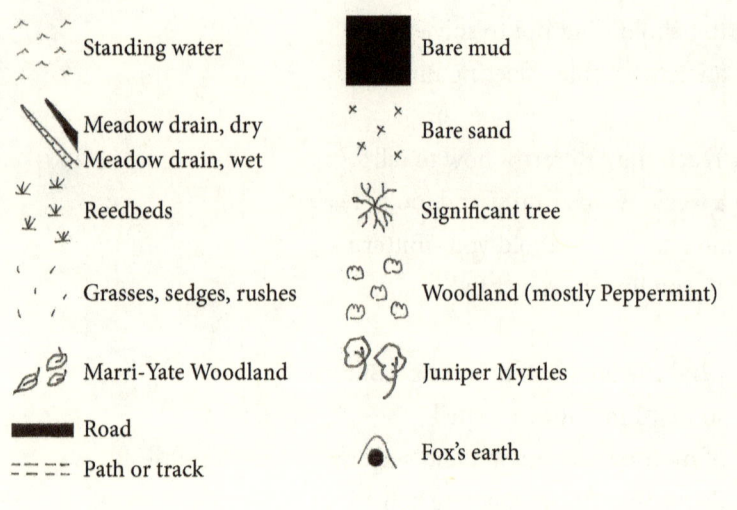

Standing water

Meadow drain, dry
Meadow drain, wet

Reedbeds

Grasses, sedges, rushes

Marri-Yate Woodland

Road

Path or track

Old farm shed

Bare mud

Bare sand

Significant tree

Woodland (mostly Peppermint)

Juniper Myrtles

Fox's earth

2. Place or sighting mentioned in text

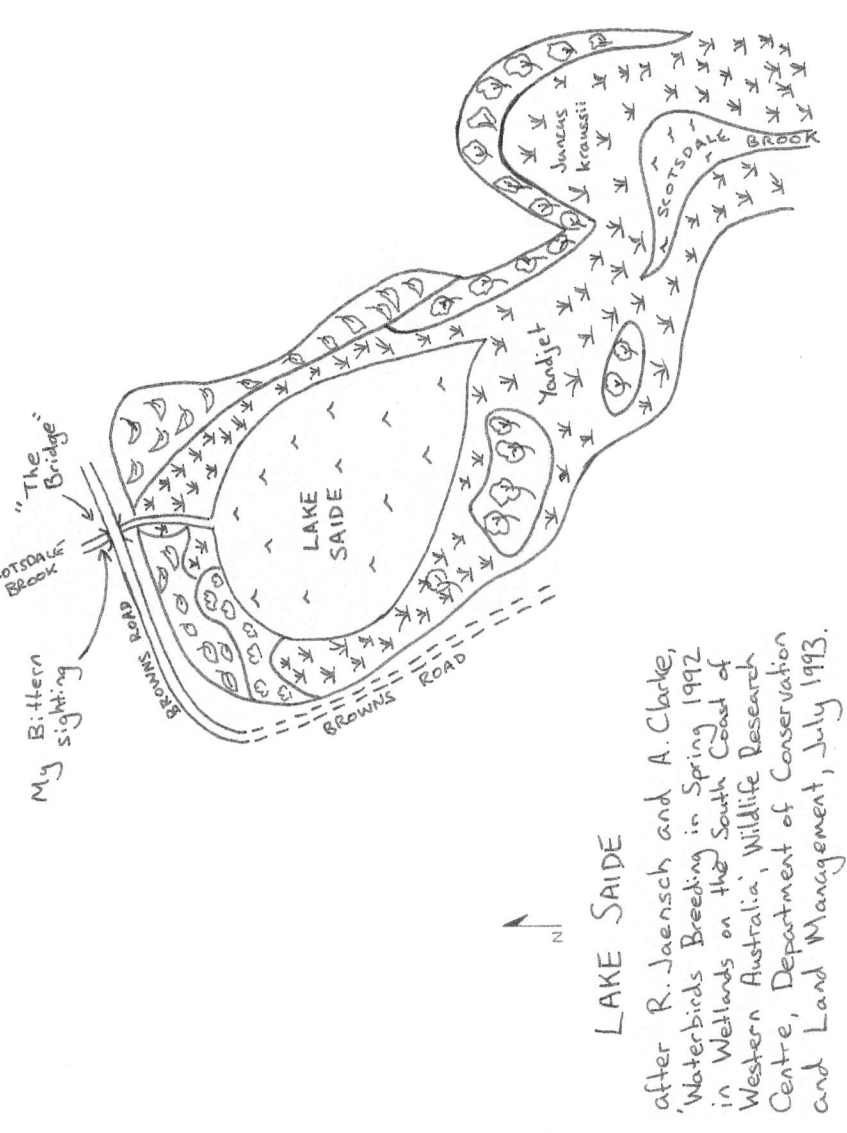

LAKE SAIDE

after R. Jaensch and A. Clarke, 'Waterbirds Breeding in Spring 1992 in Wetlands on the South Coast of Western Australia', Wildlife Research Centre, Department of Conservation and Land Management, July 1993.

11 January 2024

At home

There is a line from 'The Landrail', a poem by John Clare, which tolls in my brain whenever I think about my sighting of the Bittern. It is "[a] sort of living doubt". Clare's poem is about his attempts to see the bird which is also known as the Corncrake – now a critically endangered species which, in our own century, helped Amy Liptrot to overcome alcoholism and write what I have come to decide is one of the greatest classics of nature writing: *The Outrun*. Corncrakes helped Liptrot to defeat the urge to drink alcohol when she moved back to the Orkney Islands, in order to count them by driving around and listening out for their calls in the dead of night. Corncrakes are barometers of the health of British ecosystems. Prognosis: dire. Australasian Bitterns might well be the barometers of ours.

Corncrakes are the embodiment of doubt because, like the Bittern, they have cryptic colouration. They nest on the ground among cereal crops and hay meadows, and the reason why they are in such trouble in the twenty-first century is because changes in agricultural practices have resulted in crops being harvested earlier and earlier, so that the Corncrake has not finished raising its chicks when its cover is blown.

The Bittern I saw yesterday is "[a] sort of living doubt" for similar reasons to the Corncrake – near-perfect camouflage, and a distinctive but very different call which is heard more often than the bird is seen. But there are other reasons, too. I spend part of the morning searching all of my bird identification guides, and then ransacking the internet, for confirmation that my bird really was a Bittern. I wonder, as I do this, unable to get out of bed, whether my prodigious propensity both for doubt and for hope is itself a symptom of chronic fatigue, but eventually, I arrive at the fact that there is only one other bird for which my Bittern might have been mistaken – or vice versa: an immature Nankeen Night Heron.

I stare obsessively at pictures of them both, my blood running cold, but the process of leafing frantically through my books assuages the doubt. My bird was dark about the face; young Night Herons are not. A young Night Heron has scalloped colouration all over its back: some feathers dark brown, other feathers much lighter – it looks like a baking dish full of scalloped potatoes, a bit scorched on their skins. Bitterns' feathers are similarly bicoloured, but they are much more haphazard in their arrangement, echoing the lightness of sunlit reeds and the gathering shadows deep into the reedbeds in which they have evolved to stand, sway with the wind, and disappear. The bird I saw fitted the latter description. Nankeen Night Herons perch in trees; Bitterns do not. My bird disappeared over the trees, but it did not land in them as the Spoonbills did. I think it probably came to ground somewhere further up Scotsdale Brook, and perhaps it crept back down to fish near the bridge long after I had gone.

"A sort of living doubt". I've been one of those for years, coping with my own strangely cryptic symptoms. Coincidentally or not, today I had an appointment with the one and only local specialist in chronic fatigue. He asked me question after question for close on an hour, digging for clues that lay hidden even from me. "Chronic fatigue is a description of the symptoms, but my role is to find the cause," he said. When the questions were finished, he told me that my answers had given him two avenues to explore: sleep apnoea and fibromyalgia. He needs to investigate the sleep apnoea because I am forever waking up with a dry mouth, but I can tell that he thinks fibromyalgia is the more likely diagnosis. He tells me that fibromyalgia is usually triggered by a traumatic event, and yes, there certainly was one of those, in addition to the glandular fever. In fact, when I think about it afterwards, I realise that there were three years of trauma of one kind or another, and that the symptoms came inexorably, remorselessly in their wake.

Since then, I have tended to lurk in the shadows socially, too, and I am a bit shaken when he asks me a direct question about whether I experience social anxiety. The conversation makes me realise that all this time, I have been disguising my presence behind cryptic plumage of my own. Perhaps that is one reason why I, too, feel so at home among the reeds. Sometimes, it is necessary, socially, to come out from among them to feed in open water. Frighten me at that moment, and I too will fly up raw and ragged, galvanised by a sort of terror, my cover blown – and when I find myself back in hiding, the raggedness will have crept into my nerves, frozen me rigid, and taken possession.

12 January 2024
Browns Road, Lake Saide Road, Lee Road, Wolfes Pump Road, Eden Road, and around to Manoni Road

I want to build a better mental map of the landscape surrounding Eungedup, and especially of the flow of water across it. I won't be entering the wetland itself today, so the dogs bundle into the car with me. I cannot resist returning to the little bridge where I saw the Bittern in the hope of glimpsing it again, and this time I have a camera running as I approach, but there are only a few Black Ducks, a White-Faced Heron, a couple of White Ibises, and a Spoonbill which spots me instantly and flies straight for Lake Saide. The brook itself is not flowing – the water level is low enough that it has become a string of separate pools in places – but the water churns with fish. A group of scientists and a local Noongar elder recently surveyed the Eungedup fish population, and in addition to voracious introduced *Gambusia*s, they also found native Bluespot Gobies and Western Minnows. There are enough here to attract and tantalise a Bittern.

I can feel that my body is on the edge of its resources today, but I walk down Lee Road with the dogs, toward the locked gate of the lime mine. The hideous high fence surrounding the mine abuts on the ancient Noongar Bibbulmun Track – I restrain myself from murmuring words like *desecration*. Everywhere, at the sides of the road, there are ditches, some full of water, others choked with water-loving rushes. Large swathes of Coast Sword Sedge, their inflorescences at head-height, are all along the road. The ditches open out into the wetland I encountered on my last visit, not part of the Eungedup site, but clearly part of the complex web of water flowing – or perhaps seeping is a better word for it in this alarmingly rainless summer – between here and the estuary, Wilson Inlet, on the edge of the town of Denmark.

The day is getting warmer, and the dogs are panting, so we retrace our steps to the coolness of the car. Wilson Inlet is itself a wildlife site of international significance, so I decide to drive toward it, following the course of Scotsdale Brook. We are on Shapland Road for a while, and I realise that it runs along the brook back toward Eungedup. There is thick vegetation along its margins in places, and I assume that the Bittern must have taken shelter somewhere up here after I flushed it from under the bridge. The road is a dead end, so I turn around again, and head up Wolfes Pump Road, which rapidly becomes a bumpy and occasionally sandy track only suitable for four-wheel drives. It wends its way up and down wooded hills between two large lakes which I can only occasionally glimpse between the trees: Youngs Lake to the west, and Nenamup Inlet to the east. Once, I stop to get out and pick up a brown-barred feather with white spots, covered all over with sound-muffling velvet: a Boobook Owl's. I check Google Maps. Scotsdale Brook enters Nenamup, which is essentially a widening of it, and this water flows into Youngs Lake, which in turn communicates with the Wilson Inlet estuary.

Wilson Inlet has several tributaries – Sleeman–Cuppup River, Hay River (Genulup), the Denmark River (Kwoorabup) – but the flow of water from Eungedup also empties into the estuary. I realise that, aside from the intrinsic value of Eungedup itself, and the conservation of the Australasian Bittern and all the other wildlife I have encountered in the wetland, there is another reason why it was so essential for the community to purchase and protect Eungedup. Its water ends up in Wilson Inlet. If it becomes eutrophic, the nitrogen levels of Nenamup, Youngs Lake and Wilson Inlet will also rise, and if industrial farm chemicals enter the waters of Eungedup, they will end up here, where I am driving now, on the inland edge of the Nullaki Peninsula, along the shores of the Inlet. Moreover, as Aboriginal wisdom from across cultures in Australia teaches, wetlands like Eungedup function as the "kidneys" of the landscape, purifying its water. Saving Eungedup from drainage improves the water quality of Scotsdale Brook as it travels on through the landscape toward the sea.

It is stunningly beautiful country. Paperbarks, some of them very old, judging by the great, bulbous bases of their boles and the spongy thickness of their bark, line the shores of the Inlet. There are large, grey, knotty *Banksia* trees in the drier spaces, and occasionally the moon-mottled trunk of a Karri tree. The water, some of it Eungedup water, is wind-ruffled at present, but I have sometimes seen it so still that the reflected images of the Paperbarks are flawless, white against a cloudless sky.

I turn around again, and head rapidly across country to the Lower Denmark Road, and back again down Lake Saide Road to look for water to the east of the Manoni Road end of Eungedup's Maringup Creek. There is a significant body of water here, just outside the borders of the Eungedup site. Behind them is the vast bed of Yandjet which stretches past Maringup Creek and totally encompasses Lake Saide, but the side close to the road

is free of reeds, so I can look out across the open water, where a
flotilla of Coots is feeding on water-plants.

A large Swamp Harrier - so dark in colour
her undersides are burgundy - idly quarters
the open water. She seems indifferent - detached -
enjoying the wind in her pinions. Carelessly -
she wheels. Musk Ducks float beneath -
apparently unperturbed - she flies off north -
a great distance - until she is almost invisible -
then turns - gathers momentum - sheds altitude
in a lethal arc until she is half a tree's height
above the water - and on the edge of the Yandjet
at her sudden calamitous explosive presence
Songbirds scatter outwards like shrapnel - one bird
disappears behind her silhouette and does not
re-emerge - and she drops down far beyond
the reeds and never reappears.

       I drive back around
to Browns Road - check again for the Bittern -
the brook is empty - but as the tarmac ends
and the road curves toward Eungedup I find
Rosella feathers scattered on the gravel where
some raptor plucked them - perhaps the pierce-eyed
killer whose victim's relics I found last time
I was here. The feathers stir in wind. Their
crimson makes me shudder. There is cloud -
a tentative splash of rain. Everything else
          is silent.

I drive home - nerves jangling with exposure -
one leg aching - throbbing - tingling - struggle
against a contradictory combination of weariness
and panic - soothe myself with the thought
                              of seeping water.

※

At home in the evening, I use satellite images to trace Scotsdale Brook back to its source. It wends its way to Lake Saide through agricultural land from Lowlands, perhaps five kilometres away, where a delta of green grass marks its source. Just before its arrival at Lake Saide, the water spreads out through the Yandjet, becoming more like a fen than a brook, seeping outward to become the Eungedup wetlands. The point where the banks of Scotsdale Brook break down and this slow seepage begins is in the reedbed beyond which the Swamp Harrier flew to ground earlier today.

The farmer who grew potatoes in Eungedup had to drain the wetlands after the rainy season every year in order to plant his crop in the rich soil underneath. That is why the swollen Maringup Creek and Northwest Wetland (the wetland west of Lake Saide) still have lines of higher ground – or causeways – running through them, now mostly covered with reeds: remnants of the time when they were tilled. So, aside from the permanent open water of Lake Saide, Eungedup is a wetland in the truest sense: not lakes but literally land that is wet and sometimes – but not always – entirely under water. It has its own ebb and flow, its own seasonal seepage. I had noticed this already: there were tadpoles swimming all over Browns Road when I first started my visits, but now it is hard and dry.

This evening, again, it tries to rain and fails after a lot of wind and a few thunderclaps. Now that I have traced – in my mind, at least, and partly on the ground – the path from source to sea which is taken by Eungedup's water, I feel, as I stare at the map I have been drawing, that I can sense the wetlands' growing thirst.

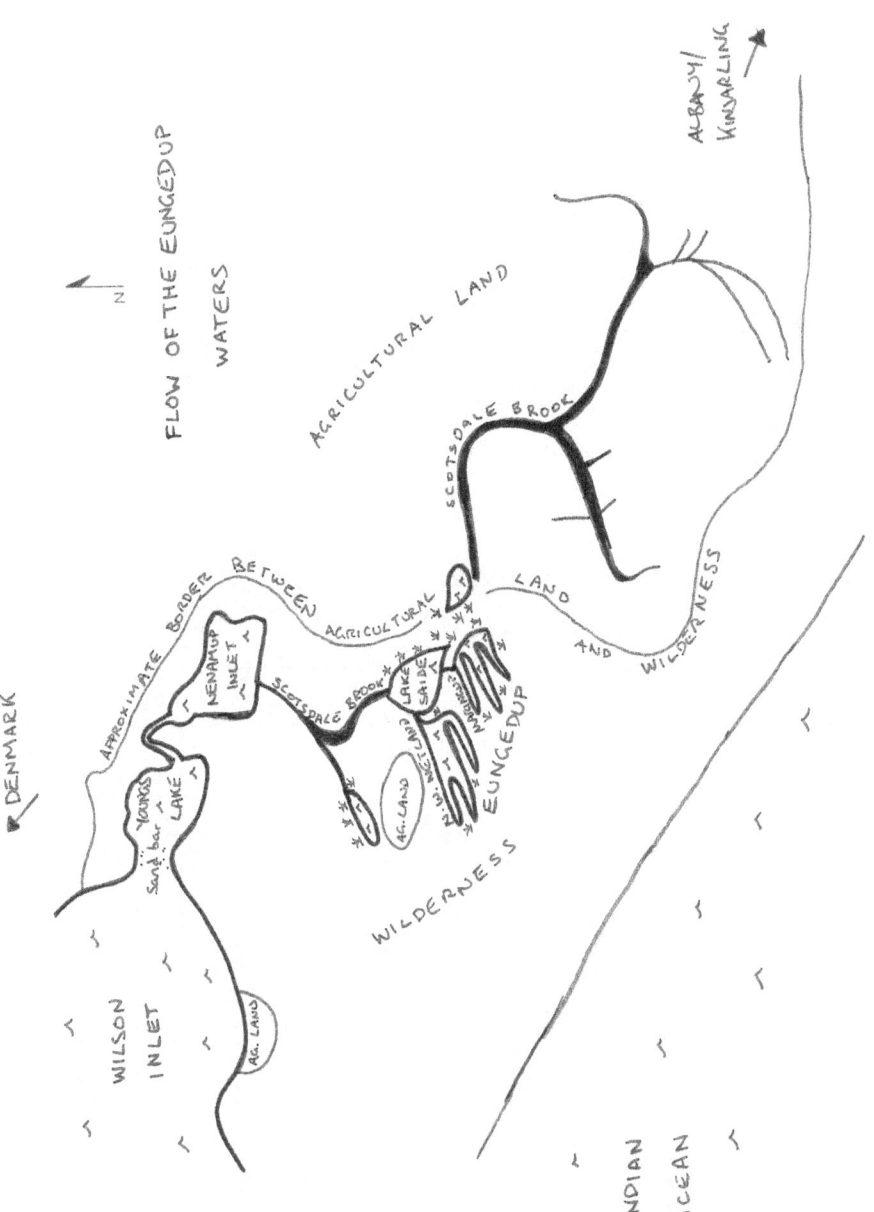

14 January 2024

*Scotsdale Brook from Browns Road toward Lake Saide,
then Browns Road to the north shore of Maringup Creek
6.05 a.m. to 8.15 a.m.*

Wood Ducks graze beside the road - not startled
when I pass them - the sky is loud with Ravens -
Redcaps and Rosellas chiming my arrival.
High up in a Juniper Myrtle four Great Egrets
survey Lake Saide - way above the living mosaic
of leathery-leafed Marri and Yate - the Paperbarks
and reeds. They have the glimpse of open water
that eludes me always - but now there's something new
to tantalise. Beside Scotsdale Brook - a wide swathe
has been mown where I can follow toward the Lake.
There are stretches where the water is all gone -
here Crakes pick about and scuttle. Silvereyes
and Fantails loop out snapping insects on the wing.
The mown sward ends in reeds - I wonder whether
I could make it further if I waded down the Brook -
so I step down on a bare patch - and in an instant
I am knee-deep in mud and sinking - flailing
after reeds - hauling myself back up on the bank.

Black and noisome mud clings to me - Eungedup mud -
veritably the living flesh of the kidneys of the catchment -
thick and dark as treacle - all that lives there rotting
down to carbon - the slick stench stays with me
and is everything of life and death - beginning - ending -
a grim turgid funk clotted on my wellingtons

and half-way up my trousers. I wipe away the worst
with handfuls of mown grass - then stride out
among the Paperbarks and their undergrowth
of rushes. The shadiest parts are bare beneath the boles -
traversed by tracks of Kangaroos. There are tidelines
of fallen branches. Damselflies dance and perch
amid the foliage - air slung with Spiders in their orbs -
hairy and red-legged - basking in sunlight at the centres
of their webs. I burst back onto Browns Road - sweaty
and frustrated. Every way I wander ends in reeds.

I do not lose my way – not physically – but among the spider-slung boles of Paperbarks with their pudgy cushions of bark and their needling little fallen leaves all over the drying mud, I feel I am losing track of myself. Although it's only early, the heat of the day is gathering, clotting at my armpits, resonating thickly with the hum of Mosquitoes. The swamp mud is already drying on my boots and on my trousers, and I have emptied most of my water bottle. In 1992, researchers fought their way through the reeds to find Lake Saide and searched for nests of Musk Ducks, Swamphens and Bitterns – the latter, of course, eluded them. They must have been wearing waders, and trampled a destructive course through the reeds in order to do so, but I have no wish to leave behind a trail.

Distraction - is a Thicket
where no path ever wound -
nor tree-fall let in sunlight
but everywhere is Wood -

no understorey grows here -
all is tangled brown -
the fallen seeds lie dormant
where Thought has never - grown -

and where there is no Centre
and no Extremity -
the Word is formed by formlessness
and Voice is never - me -

but Birds - who know each Tree apart -
as Adjective - or Noun -
will sing the Verb - Identify -
though I am but - Anon -

And that, of course, is what is supposed to happen: I need to be defeated by the Paperbarks and reeds, for Lake Saide is not mine to reach. Eungedup teaches many lessons – humility is one of them.

It's cloudless - and out upon Browns Road - I start
to swelter - the way is dry - and coloured with red clover.
Tau Emeralds - a second generation - dart and shimmer.

Australian Shelduck
Tadorna tadornoides

Under the Yandjet - Shelducks are worrying
zitting and zeeking - threshing their wings -

suddenly Sheldrakes are whickering over -
breasted with chestnut - flying in throngs.

Wings are white-flashes - one Shelduck before them
worrying still - in a rush to be gone -
whizzing and buzzing - the Sheldrakes are honking
'til all disappear - in the dazzling sun.

On the nearside bank of Maringup a Tiger Snake is basking, slowly wending, leading me the way that I was walking. In shadows of a Peppermint she finds seclusion – easing all her length into the shadows.

I climb my Tree and wait. A pair of Pelicans floats idly. A Swan passes above me, wide pinions backlit by an intensifying sun. Far off in the wetland, a Raptor sits unmoving, watching. Little Cormorants – perching on their own tree skeleton – hang their wings out to dry. Tau Emeralds scud above the water, seeking nuptials.

From an overhanging Peppermint
          a Sacred Kingfisher
                    swoops straight down
            to water -
     flies up triumphant
         with a fish's long thin gleam
                 trailing from his bill -

            thrashes it against a branch -
      seems to fly away -

                        then reappears
        upon a higher bough -
                        the long fish still uneaten -
        smacks it hard again
                        systematically smashing
        the whole skeleton -
                then swallows - sits upright -

turns his back upon me -
                begins at once to preen
        splaying out one wing
                        tucking his head under
                rearranging feathers -
                        reaching backwards
        dabbling at his tail-base -
                fanning his other wing.

He reaches out a leg -
                cocks his head
                        and scratches -
        bends wing to breast
                        and nibbles
                                with his bill-tip -
        flicks his plumage -
                is in no hurry -
                        listens to Cockatoos -
        flits down to a dead branch
                        over water -
        turns around to face me -
                snips at his breast feathers -

stares downward -
>   lifts and flicks his tail
>   twists -
>   fights with a twig -
>   looses a white dropping
>   which splashes into water -

sits absorbing sky-colour -
>   suddenly drops -
>   hits the surface -
>   snaps up
>   a Dragonfly nymph -
>   and on an old dead branch
>   thrashes twice and splits it
>   tosses it upwards - snapping -
>   gulps it down -

strops his bill against the wood -
>   whets it -
>   cleanses it of mud -

and again he hits the water -
>   this time unsuccessful -
>   shoots up higher - perches -
>   whetting
>   preening
>   scratching -

is interrupted
>   by a pair of Wrens

                their tails erect
        and scolding.

Now - a Reed Warbler
        is in the branches
                also preening.

Silvereyes
        surround me.

Sacred Kingfisher
Todiramphus sanctus

Sacred Kingfisher - coloured like water
over white sand - immaculate watcher -
waiting for Minnows - or Mosquito Fish -
preens for a minute - then drops in a flash -
plummets to water - with barely a splash -
emerges triumphant - scarcely awash -
holds up his catch - scales a-glinting -
gives its limp form an absolute thrashing -
gobbles and preens himself - pauses to scratch
not once neglecting - to stare and to watch -
ready to plunge - or to hide by a leaf -
flies off like cobalt kindled to Life.

⚘

Brad and Jill Kneebone have invited me to visit them at their home in Lowlands, only minutes away by car from Eungedup, so with my spirits still leaping after watching the Sacred Kingfisher, I drop by on my way home. The house is set well back from the road, at the end of a grassy track, only a short stroll away from what Google Maps calls Scotsdale Brook, and Brad calls simply "the drain". No matter what it is called, it is one of the main channels of Eungedup's catchment. We sit outside, and Jill plies us with coffee and beautiful fruitcake, the scent of which seems instantly to beckon a sleek and immaculately feathered tribe of Splendid Fairywrens who, totally unafraid, approach right up to our chairs to peck at crumbs, swaying their generous tails and looking like animated Byzantine mosaics in the sunlight.

Brad has wise eyes and a kindly manner. He seems not at all surprised to see me caked from the thighs down with reeking Eungedup mud – a smell with which he has long been familiar – and is totally unperturbed when I tell him how I came to be so bespattered. Who wouldn't almost drown oneself in cloying, decomposing silt, simply to catch a glimpse of Lake Saide?

We talk for a long time about our shared obsession. He brings out a magnificent table-sized aerial photograph of Eungedup, its catchment, and the waterways that lead to Wilson Inlet. I pore over it in a state of transported delight. I can see the precise position of every reedbed, and blue lines mark the directions of the channels which, until around seven years ago, the farmer used to drain the wetlands into Lake Saide. Brad points out the places where I can find overgrown paths into different parts of Eungedup, and speaks of having paddled around in his kayak among the reedbeds – even on Lake Saide. This fills me with a desperate longing. He has tested the depths of the water: fifty to eighty centimetres in many places – the bitterns need it shallower for their feeding.

Conversation shifts inevitably to Tiger Snakes. I tell him of the two I saw today – the second was lying quite still on Browns Road with its neck flattened, just as I was leaving, and I wondered for a moment whether it had been run over, until I moved to pass it by and it woke out of its sun-spangled daze, took one bleary look at me, and made for cover. Brad recounts a time when he wasn't wearing wellingtons or waders – just a pair of loose trousers – and felt something tugging from behind. He thought at first it must be a Bobtail Lizard, but actually, it was a Tiger Snake, angry because he'd trodden on its tail. It sank its fangs into the material, then fled. All of this is narrated in a tone of utmost respect – and indeed of sorrow for the inadvertent treading. If Snakes really wanted to get us, we'd all have been envenomed long ago.

A plump Quenda appears and disappears. Blood-red Dragonflies – Scarlet Perchers – haunt the garden. Brad leads me around to the back of the house, and there – to my astonishment and delight – is a thriving wetland of his own – a broad pond filled with the same waters that fill Eungedup, fringed with similar vegetation, and everywhere, there are Dragonflies. A pair of them are flying in tandem, the female dangling and dipping her abdomen in the water. Brad draws my attention to the back wall of the house. All over it, there are the discarded carapaces of Dragonfly nymphs, still clinging to the concrete. Brad tells me he has watched them emerging. Sometimes they do so, only to be snapped up instantly by birds.

The pond has its own breeding family of Coots, some of whom are busily upending, and further off, a Musk Duck is idly floating. A Pied Cormorant sits and elongates its neck. Brad reminisces about the day an Osprey plucked a trout out of this water. He has seen Hobbies hawking for Dragonflies, looping down over the surface, and once there was a Square-Tailed Kite. At night, the frog chorus is so loud that doors have to be closed in order to concentrate on anything else. As he is talking, an immature Buff-Banded Rail emerges, and starts foraging right in front of us, oblivious to our presence. He and Jill have been watching it ever since it was a vulnerable, fluffy, ebony-coloured chick. The wetland he has created isn't perfect, he tells me; if he were to do it again, some things would be different. But under a completely cloudless sky, with shimmering mirages starting to form in the distance, and the blood-red Dragonflies scudding, this is one place on Earth where I could kid myself – if only for one fleeting moment – that mass extinction isn't happening, and human beings and wild things are at peace.

꙳

At home this evening - although I've washed
my clothes and bathed and scrubbed - I sit writing
and I swear I still can smell it - rich - clotted - glorious
mud of Eungedup - stinking slick Mother of Crakes

and Kingfishers - Damselflies and Dragonflies -
Black Swans and Tiger Snakes. I rifle through
my things, seeking out that stench - it's nowhere
and in everything - clinging - perhaps - to beard
or nostril-hairs. All these months - its odour soaking in -
mud
    of Eungedup -
  underneath
      my
skin.

19 January 2024
At home

Days when I am not able to visit Eungedup – because I haven't got the strength – bring an all-pervasive sense of loss. The memory of the Kingfisher – streaking to the water and rising up triumphant, shedding droplets, bill clamped tightly on the long silver arc of a fish's body – becomes a focus of a yearning that almost spirals into mourning. If only I could raise some magic to transport me out there, I think, I would be content just to wedge myself in the crook of my climbing-Tree with my binoculars, and stay there all day and well into the night.

It is dangerous, when I am in this state, to read the news, but today when I do so, there is something a little heartening. Australia's Minister for the Environment has blocked a proposal to drain a massive, ecologically significant wetland in Victoria for the purposes of building a wind farm which could easily be constructed on land that is not wilderness. She must have felt vindicated in this decision when, just a few days afterwards, the Sharp-Tailed Sandpiper, which uses the wetland, was added to the national threatened species list. It gives me hope that she may respond in the same way in a few months to a longstanding and hotly contested attempt to "develop" another wetland in Queensland, a feeding-stop for Eastern Curlews and other endangered species of migratory wading birds.

The Sharp-Tailed Sandpiper has been recorded by the Denmark Bird Group as a visitor to Eungedup, too. How wonderful it would be, I find myself fantasising, if even a few people in positions of great power were to feel the sense of wonder, yearning and loss that many other, less powerful people feel when they contemplate the richness of wild habitats, and reel with dizzy sickness at the prospect of their degradation or destruction. If anything in life is a motivation for joy and wonder, then surely it is the knowledge that there are birds a fraction of the weight of my own heart – birds who fly, without technological assistance, or even a compass, from Siberia to Australia and back again, in some cases with a single stop-over in the Yellow Sea, and in others without pausing at all – and that you or I may see these living miracles with our own eyes – perhaps even pick up a feather one of them has dropped – knowing that in a matter of weeks, these tiny balls of plumpness and plumage, impervious even to ocean gales, will be breeding on the opposite side of the world.

An Edge of Bill - to catch the Glint -
A Tilt - into the Sun -
An Eye that sees the arching World -
The Distance - to begin -

A Compass Blade - inside a Mind -
A Sextant - in a Brain -
A Pulse - that finds Magnetic North -
A Voice - of wilding Song -

Legs that fold - for Hemispheres
To touch down in the Froth -
An ear that turns - to hear the Whelk -
A Heart - that plumbs the Earth -

And surely, no one, contemplating that living glory, could be immune to the abiding grief that comes with knowing that it is precisely *our* generation that has caused the catastrophic decline of these species which have pre-existed ours by millions of years – that *we* are responsible for leaving a world bereft.

Often when I lie awake at night, having given up on the possibility of sleep, my mind retraces the path up from my climbing-Tree on the shore of Maringup Creek, which leads past the gnarled *Banksia* tree to the little hill among the Peppermint woodland where Dragonflies have perches, and where once I saw the Sun Moth and the Sand Wasp. There is wonder here too, amid the undergrowth, that I wish it were possible to communicate to mining executives, "developers" and politicians. The moment when a Blue Skimmer – entirely dependent for its whole existence on this tiny little tessary in the mosaic of land and water – settles with splayed wings on a broken twig, and sits tight as you approach it, until you can see the diaphanous spaces between the wing veins, and the darker spots in the world-encompassing orbs of its eyes, is one of the purest and most joyful moments that can happen in a human life. The destruction of such places cuts to the heart – it is the unacknowledged bereavement which is the fundamental, largely undiagnosed, illness ravaging the human species in the early twenty-first century.

Sometimes it feels as though chronic fatigue, or fibromyalgia, or whatever my ultimate diagnosis ends up being, is the way that yearning – grief confronting the enormity of mass extinction – expresses itself. Edward O. Wilson, in *The Diversity of Life*, points out that it has taken the natural world tens of millions of years to recover from previous extinction events, and it is therefore vain and irresponsible to console ourselves with the idea that nature will replace what our species is destroying. In human terms, extinction means that when it is gone, it is gone, and we all lie bereft in our beds, staring up at a blank ceiling, justifiably deprived of sleep.

I think of the Lichen growing on the gnarled old *Banksia*. It is fruticose in form, sprouting out from the bark in strands and tufts – a member of the group of Lichens that is most sensitive to pollution. Long may it grow there – the air of Eungedup free of our invisible poisons. Pinned down in my yearning and exhaustion, I know at least that by buying Eungedup and saving it from draining and development, we have given its inhabitants – right down to the lichen – a fighting chance.

Bole-bark - green leaf - Lichen - rock -
Are fundamental truths -
There is no culture can usurp
The reign of Undergrowth -

Though we rage at it and raze -
And cry - Eradicate -
Bole-bark - green leaf - Lichen - rock -
Are staunch - and they can wait -

And wait - and wait - to reign - again
When sovereignty is ceded -
From the Land which ruled us - all -
It's we who have been - weeded -

20 January 2024
At home

Not so long ago, doctors would have been telling me that the very last thing on Earth that I should do, given my state of health, was to develop an obsession for visiting a "swamp". Nineteenth century theories about contagion still clung to the notion that illness was caused not by microorganisms, but by "miasma" – vapours emanating from rotting organic material, like the stench that followed me around the day I stepped into the mud of Scotsdale Brook. The notion itself was often advanced as a justification for draining wetlands, and the persistence of that noun, "swamp", in the vocabularies of those in the present day who want to profit from the further destruction of wetlands, is a way of playing on a range of fears that are unnatural, but which in western cultures have been so exacerbated by propaganda that they have become instinctive.

The fallacy of the dangerous effects of "miasma" has a long history that can be traced at least as far back as the writings of the Roman architectural expert, Vitruvius:

> For when the morning breezes blow toward the town at sunrise, if they bring with them mist from marshes and, mingled with the mist, the poisonous breath of creatures to be wafted into the bodies of the inhabitants, they will make the site unhealthy.

There were two possible responses to belief in this dogma: one could avoid planning towns in the vicinity of wetlands, or one could drain the wetlands and build the towns regardless. Nothing much had changed when colonisers in the nineteenth century sought to justify the draining of the complex wetland system that once clustered around Perth's Swan River, recently stolen from its Noongar custodians. The *Perth Inquirer* opined in August 1873:

> When it is borne in mind that Perth has no natural drainage – that percolation and evaporation do for it what sewers do for other [...] more populated cities; that the river upon whose banks it is built has no appreciable tide, and that many acres around us in all directions are covered with marsh and bog, producing foetid, unwholesome miasma, all the year round, it is indeed matter for wonder how it is that pestilential fever is not for ever stalking in our midst.

Wetlands are, of course, associated with microbial diseases spread by Mosquitoes: malaria in tropical zones, Murray Valley encephalitis – a virus which lives in the bodies of herons, especially Nankeen Night Herons, and Cormorants, and is transmitted to humans by Mosquitoes – and the Ross River virus, which is also spread by Mosquitoes from animals to humans. It might be possible to contract aspergillosis by breathing in fungal spores in wetlands – birds can certainly contract it. But the notion of a creeping "miasma" – a sort of ghostly emanation of the wetland, is itself only a symptom of the pathological fear of wilderness which has caused a far more frightening pandemic: the worldwide collapse of ecosystems, and especially the mosaics of habitats associated with wetlands, as a result of human activity.

My reading on "miasma" today reminds me of other cultural phenomena that reinforce a fear of "swamps". I think of nursery bogies like the evil water-faerie, Jenny Greenteeth, who supposedly haunts the wetlands of Scotland, waiting to catch children by their ankles and drag them under, so that she can devour them. I think too of the setting of *The Hound of the Baskervilles* in another kind of wetland, the Grimpen Mire (based on the Foxtor Mires on Dartmoor), and the way, despite that novel's naturalistic explanation for its "spectral hound", Sir Arthur Conan Doyle is able to build an atmosphere of terror around a water-soaked setting and images of phosphorescence and rising mist. In popular culture, I think of *Creature from the Black Lagoon*, and I reflect on the fact that when I search for documentaries on Australian wetlands on streaming services, every one of them has as its focus lurking predators in places like the Daintree: crocodiles who snatch unassuming humans and devour them; even leeches who vampirise unsuspecting crabs. Here in Australia, we have our own nursery bogey, too: the Bunyip, derived ultimately from Aboriginal legends, but infantilised by the colonisers into a malevolent spirit, its death-moans conflated with the booming of the Bittern.

But I think also of the legend of the Tiddy Mun, a faerie from the Lincolnshire Fens in England, who was a benevolent spirit of the wetland landscape, until the fens were drained and he suddenly turned exceptionally nasty, causing cattle to die, pigs to pine and starve, and children to waste away and expire. He had to be appeased with magical rituals before his wrath was assuaged: one of the most striking folkloric admissions that when we drain wetlands, we invite a terrible vengeance.

The true vengeance may not be the unexpected deaths of children and farm animals, but there is certainly a soul-destroying inheritance that blights humanity in a landscape devoid of wetlands, or one in which all of them are eutrophic and poisoned with farm chemicals. Yet we "environmentalists" still meet with the "miasma" myth when we try to defend what remains of our ravaged wetland ecosystems. We are told that "wetland" is just a euphemism for "swamp", that wetlands are useless to humanity, and that their water is "needed" for agriculture – even as those same wetlands are purifying the water poisoned by irresponsible agricultural practices.

The ignorance of settlers who heard Bitterns booming, and concluded that swamps must be either drained or avoided because of Bunyips, really was the deepest form of ignorance, because a closely related species of Bittern booms in Britain too. It is an ignorance which persists, and that can only be fought by communicating the wonder and delight which is the real experience of visiting a place like Eungedup, and by reminding the world that for indigenous cultures across the globe, wetlands are oases – sources of food and sites of healing. Even the Yandjet itself has roots, *yanjidi*, which our local Noongar people pounded for their pulpy goodness and baked in cakes, and its fibrous parts provided materials for making string for baskets. For them, the rivers, streams and wetlands were lovingly gouged out of the landscape by the gigantic Wagyl serpent, and the human beings were charged with the responsibility not to "subdue the creation", as in Judeo-Christian tradition, but to be "the Carers of Everything": to nurture and celebrate wetlands, not to encourage the population, from childhood, to irrationally fear their mists so that no one would protest when farmers or developers decided to drain them for profit. The working people of the Lincolnshire Fens worked this out, too. In their desperate attempts to assuage the grief of the Tiddy Mun for his drained and ravaged habitat, they chanted:

Tiddy Mun, wi'out a name
White heed, walkin' lame
While the watter teems tha fen
Tiddy Mun'll harm none.

But "miasma" is a medical myth which has maintained its destructive potency and aura of paranoia for more than two thousand years. It is not a concept that is likely to dissipate in a hurry. What if we were to reclaim it, and mobilise it against the destruction?

I fear a grey Miasma
that penetrates the Soul -
a spiritual Effluvium
disgorged - by poisoned Soil -

a Fog - of hazy thinking
in dim - Eutrophic minds -
that hovers over wetlands
and withers them - with Winds -

that parches what was Teeming
that withers what was Wild

that replicates - a Dustbowl
and clogs up - all the World -

that clouds the shallow Waters
so Birds can't see - to fish -
infects the Streams and Estuaries
and where the Breakers wash -

I fight a grey Miasma -
I wriggle from its grip -
And all I have for weapons
Are Wonder - Heart - and Hope -

21 January 2024
North shore of Maringup Creek
8 a.m. to 12.30 p.m.

I have an hour before I am due to meet with a group of volunteers who are going to assist Mark Parre – an expert on revegetating sites that have been overtaken by weeds – in gathering seeds of reeds and sedges. It is unusual for me to be in a hurry when I am at Eungedup, but I am anxious to climb my Tree on the shore of Maringup Creek –

not too hurried - though - to miss noticing
a Red-Eared Firetail darting down Browns Road
among the Wrens - a flare of sudden brightness
receding as I walk - but when I pause beside
my chapels - the Reed Warblers are strangely
silent. I jog up through the woodland - slow down
toward my Tree - and this time there is no desperate
scuttle of Birds across the water. They have grown
accustomed to me - or perhaps I'm getting better
at arriving.

A Pelican stands
on a reed island -
 right side lit by sun -
unwieldy bill
preening his breast
with surprising delicacy.

Two Black Ducks are upending -
as they slip back
upright
the water runs gleaming
down their iridescent
speculums - runnels
      along their arching necks -

                                                dribbles
                                                off
                                                their
                                                bills -

a third Black Duck stands
      on a waterlogged stump
            surrounded
          by reeds and water
      mirroring the Pelican -
            preening -
a fourth sits - half dozing
          beside her
                on a raised lump
                of mud -

a Swamphen
      stalks behind
           a thin line of reeds -
regards me
      first with one eye
           then with the other
      flits her tail -
           flashing

       the white underside -
            decides
                  not to flee.

The Pelican drifts
       with a mate
            far out on the water -
   one opens wings -
            flaps them idly -
       stretches
            the stiffness
       out of them -
               paddles
                     aimlessly -

into full sunlight - both Birds
    carrying their wings
        half-raised
            above their bodies
       curled
           like furling sails.

On a distant roosting-tree
      a single Spoonbill
           completes
         with the arc of his back
                and neck
        the barkless curves
      of the branch where he
is perching -

        his whiteness reflected
                in the curved breast
                        of the Pied Cormorant
        beside him.

The Swamphen
        is now floating -
                with every paddle
                        his white patch
                              flashing.

A family of Wrens
        has joined me
                in my Tree
                      picking lerp
from the undersides
        of leaves - accompanying
                their hunting
with little tweezering songs
        snipping at the morning.

All but one are females
        or immatures -
                joined by a Fantail
        living up to his name
posturing his plumes -
        spreading them and scolding -
                proud of his
                        domain.

Time has run away from me, so I am about to start hurrying back down Browns Road to meet Mark Parre and his group of volunteers – giving a wide berth to a hunting Tiger Snake – when a four-wheel drive with a Wilson Inlet Catchment Committee insignia appears on the path in front of me. Tim Gamblin, the Biodiversity Project Officer, gives me a lift back to the top of Browns Road for the briefing. He has an expansive smile and an evident love for his work and for the wetlands. A Quenda hurries across the track in front of us – the first I have seen here, although they turn up all the time in our garden – his back characteristically hunched, eyes like glistening beads, whiskers quivering in his hurry. It is the first time I have seen Eungedup from inside a vehicle – a view slightly higher above the reeds. Everything swoops past in a moment: the gnarled *Banksia* where the Harrier sometimes likes to perch, the muddy little platform behind the reeds where the Crakes and Rails come to eat – now dry and hardening in the heat – the wider opening in the reeds which leads to the grassy pathway to the old farm building in the middle of the Northwest Wetland. All those jewelled moments whip past me in an instant.

When we arrive, a Western Spinebill is flying from shrub to shrub, searching for blossoms, and a group of about a dozen human enthusiasts has gathered. I am distracted from some of the conversations, my eyes drawn to the long, sickle-curved bill, plying for nectar with a feathery tongue. Shaun Ossinger is talking about the recent history of Eungedup. It had been farmed for potatoes for decades until, in 2019, the sandbank at

Wilson Inlet was not artificially opened as it is normally, and suddenly the watertable was much higher than it normally was – banked all the way up Scotsdale Brook back to Eungedup. In this situation, *Typha* – the Yandjet – took immediate advantage, growing in such profusion and density that when the farmer came to flatten the reedbeds with his tractor as he had always done, it proved an impossible obstacle. The "bulrush" seed heads clogged his radiator. The farmer retreated – the *Typha* inexorably advanced – the Bitterns returned. The first skirmish of the oncoming battle had been won by wilderness.

Tim has placed audio recorders and cameras at key spots in the wetlands, and the booming of three breeding male Bitterns has been recorded this summer. His cameras have picked up a family of Rakalis, but also Foxes, one of whom emerges in the camera frame, wet and muddy. It has been swimming – a distinct threat to Bitterns. He confirms that some mysteriously large burrows I have found in the woodlands are Foxes' earths. My mind wanders back to the *Typha* – the Bitterns' secure retreat from human beings, and hopefully from Foxes and Harriers.

We walk back to the grassy area between the wetlands. Over the next few hours, my understanding of this weedy plot, so beloved of hunting Tiger Snakes, is to be transformed. As Mark Parre starts explaining his plans for the area, there is discussion of the *Typha orientalis* itself. This species of Yandjet, which is all over Eungedup, was once thought to be introduced, and could be eradicated without a permit – but archaeological pollen cores proved this assumption incorrect. Mark suggests that

Eungedup was probably originally dominated by the Jointed Twig Rush, *Baumea articulata*, before the Yandjet took over. One of the volunteers asks why, if Yandjet is native, it hadn't taken over long before. No doubt it is because nitrogen run-off from farms favours the Yandjet, but to the Bitterns and the other water birds, it hardly seems to matter. In coming years, though, its growth may need to be controlled, so that it does not engulf every bit of open water. It is the mosaic of reeds and open water which is so perfect for the wildlife of Eungedup, and if human activity has encouraged the Yandjet, human beings may also need to curtail its spread.

Mark has other, more pressing goals in mind, relating to the eradication of invasive species. The green space where we are now standing used to be potato-growing land – the whole swathe of it. Now, about a half of it is covered with Kikuyu Grass, an invasive weed – although the Tiger Snakes seem to have adapted to it – and an assortment of introduced docks, thistles and willowherbs. These are wildflowers in the country where I once spent eighteen years of my life, but here, they are dangers to biodiversity, spreading clouds of windblown seeds. The other half of the area, near to the two *Banksia* trees, is covered with native reeds and sedges. Mark explains that this is because, in winter, the meadow is partially inundated. Kikuyu cannot survive with its rhizomes under water for too long, so natural inundation gives the native species a chance.

The meadow suddenly strikes me as a field of battle between ancient sedges and agricultural weeds – the fortunes of the opposing armies affected not only by rainfall, but also by the hydrology of the artificial drainage system that was dug into the landscape when the wetlands were a farm. In one corner of the meadow, overrun with vegetation and fallen into disrepair, is a corrugated tin shed, which Tim tells us was once the old pump house: the waters of Eungedup were not simply allowed to seep into Lake Saide through the drainage system – they were actively pumped away. As a result of the sudden end to that pumping regime in 2019, the natural wetland vegetation has slowly begun to recover, advancing across the field.

Mark proposes to facilitate its advance. We will collect the seeds of the Rushes – twenty percent of the current yield – so that they can be used to actively revegetate the rest of this area. He leads us out into the meadow, among the chest-high Rushes. First, we will work individually to gather seeds of the Marsh Club Rush, *Bolboschoenus caldwellii*. The seed capsules are clumped around the stems, four or five of them together, each about the size and colour of a peanut with the rusty skin still attached. Slide the stem in between your fingers, pull gently upwards, and the capsules fall into your hand. Crush them a little with your thumb, and instantly, they disintegrate into chaff which blows away in the wind as you hold them up, leaving a surprising quantity of seeds, greenish-gold, the size and shape of teardrops. Their lightness nestles against your skin. We step out among the clumps of reeds, watching for Snakes, and make our harvest, dropping the seeds into brown paper bags.

But the seed capsules themselves are little habitats in their own right. There are three species of Spider amid the gleanings: a tiny Crab Spider with an unwieldy oblong abdomen, a larger species with an elongated body and, between the reed stems, the occasional fantastically plump, yellow Orb Spider. I find myself pausing before I pluck each head of seeds, searching for Spiders, but they still end up in the brown paper bags, and Mark promises that all of them will be left open under the reeds after our work, so that any accidentally imprisoned Spiders can escape. I look more closely, and discover that we have also inadvertently made a harvest of swarms of black Beetles the size of pinheads.

Next, we work on the Great Soft Rush, *Juncus pallidus*. These are much taller – above head height, and their seed heads are more numerous, and considerably smaller. It takes two people working together to collect these seeds, and Mark works with me. I must concentrate on holding a bucket, above the level of the introduced dock plants, so that none of their seeds fall into the bucket. Mark bends the inflorescences into the bucket, and pats them with his hand, or knocks them gently against the side. When I look inside the bucket, there is dark-brown powder at the bottom of it: thousands of miniscule seeds, which have fallen out of slits in the seed heads. Only the seeds that are ripe on a particular day will fall when they are given this treatment, so we can be less strict on only taking twenty percent of these. It is a very low-impact harvest. I lick the end of my finger, pick up a smear of the seeds, and look at them closely through the reverse end of my binoculars – an old trick I learned for when I have forgotten to bring a hand lens. The individual seeds are still scarcely discernible. They are so fine that they blow away easily in the wind. The slightest breeze might create a whirlwind in the bucket and whisk them away.

Reed seeds shedding - ready to lift
like smoke - or flowing like water -
tiny receptacles - life within motes -
eddying - waiting for winter -

Reed seeds - may you fall on bare earth
with nothing to shroud you - in shadow -
shaken to freedom - winnowed by wind -
setting your roots - in the shallow -

As we work, Mark tells me about his past. He worked in construction until 1990, but when he felt that nail guns were becoming more important than the craft itself, he decided that he wanted to work for the environment, and did a certificate in horticulture. It was not a surprising decision for someone who had grown up on a farm at the edge of the Stirling Range National Park, Koi Kyeunu-ruff – an astonishing mountain ecosystem with more endemic species than almost anywhere else in the world. In 1993, working for the Shire of Denmark, he was building a revegetation nursery and seedbank: a six-month program that resulted in the growing of ten thousand native plants, and the collection of a large seed repository. That six-month stint turned into a thirty-year career which is technically ending now with his retirement, but I detect no waning of his enthusiasm for the work. He has spent the past year training his replacement.

It seems to me that Mark has lived an enchanted thirty years under the spell of the glorious potential of seeds. At home, he grows food plants – feijoas, and especially blueberries. He collects the seeds from blueberries purchased in shops, but when they grow, the plants that emerge are throwbacks to natural types. It is a fascinating and delicious hobby.

After half an hour, our bin has less than a quarter of a brown paper bagful of seed in it – but that constitutes millions upon millions of seeds, and Mark's intention is that these ones will not be cast to the wind to take their chances. They will need to be grown first in a nursery. Direct seeding doesn't work if there are plants that will overshadow the seedlings, and Kikuyu rapidly covers everything. If you remove the Kikuyu, the same land will be covered with thistles the next year. In a nutrient-rich environment, the weeds have everything in their favour, and Mark freely admits that he is still working out what will be the best strategy for giving the reeds their best chance in their battle with the weeds.

I have been hearing rumours that there is an old well in the corner of this meadow. We tramp off looking for it, brambles catching at our trousers and scratching our hands. I am astonished that no one has seen a Snake – I know already how many of them there are here, but they have sensibly made themselves scarce. It takes some time for anyone to find the well, but eventually there is a shout, and we all come over to look. It is covered on all sides by weeds, with others growing out of the middle of it, and it is surrounded by a ring of concrete – the water perhaps fifty centimetres below the surface of the soil. The water looks surprisingly clear and fresh.

I walk back and crush another seed capsule of *Bolboschoenus*, letting the seeds trickle out of my hand and onto a patch of bare soil. The seeds seem to fall like water – emulating the thing that gives them life. It is water that will be the secret weapon in this war between the rushes and the weeds – victory by seepage. The Kikuyu will soon be in retreat, and then the whole of Eungedup will be either woodland or wetland –

wetland
wet land -
watersoaked soil -
spiked all over
with the serried
spears of reeds -
and everywhere
there will be perfect spaces
for a Bittern
to raise her eyes and bill to sky -
sway slightly in the breeze -
stay - and -

        disappear -

23 January 2024

*The path to the farm shed in the Northwest Wetland,
and the north shore of Maringup Creek
4.35 p.m. to 8.17 p.m.*

Tomorrow is my first day back at school. The sky is cloudless – my mood – is difficult to define. A bushfire near Walpole has left a smoky haze that lingers on the horizon.

Here I know I am on the territory of Tiger Snakes and not of human beings - this scarcely discernible track of knee-high grass into the wetland - where Snakes are only vulnerable from sky. I've strapped protective gaiters up above my knees - tucked them in my boots - and found myself a stick to part the grass before me as I walk. Sometimes stems stir strangely up ahead of me - I catch my breath - but only wind is pulsing.

      Through the reeds - I sometimes glimpse the open water. There are more Swamphens out here than I imagined - some stalking at the mud's edge - one perching at head height - trampling the stems.

I pass on through the long green corridor of Yandjet - stopping only to scoop a Damselfly upon my finger - Aurora Bluetail with a bright orange body and wings which seem too tiny to bear him up in flight - then step out in front of open water. A flock of Grey Teals have not yet noticed me. They dabble with their heads

just below the surface - turn amidships - waggle tails -
flow away without flushing.

                        The water level's fallen
since the last time I came here - a wide expanse of silt
surrounds the lake - every inch embossed with prints
of Waterbirds. Straw-Necked Ibises fly above me - I count
more than fifty - then a startled gaggle of another ten -
behind them - a Harrier's swooping - rapidly closing -
thirty Shelducks loop frantically over water - stirred up
by the Raptor. Spoonbills too are lifting - flapping -
scattering - a Pelican loudly rattling - all of them
hugging in their flight the contours of land and water -
but the Harrier - loses interest - soars onward toward
Maringup. The Spoonbills return to their roosting-tree -
the Shelducks and the Ibises find the water.

                                Soon I find
I'm standing where last time a Tiger Snake was hunting
in the growing grass beside the old farm shed
in the middle of the wetland. Beneath the rafters -
old Swallows' nests - and darker patches in the wood
where ancient nests have fallen. Sun glints through
the roofing. The Harrier returns - but scuds off
when a Sea Eagle cleaves between a flock of Spoonbills
splicing it through the centre. The Eagle swoops straight
through them - and suddenly the sky's aboil
with Cormorants and Egrets - Shelducks whirling
in a turmoil - hurling down to water - rising on
the updrafts. A Spoonbill lifts alarmed - turns her long

impossible head and bill toward the Eagle - but
the raptor's lost all interest - soaring to the northward -
and the mad stir of birds dwindles and subsides.

I am deeper in the wetland than I've ever been before.
The mud is a manuscript - covered with illuminations
and palimpsests left by birds' feet: great initials left
by Swamphens walking toward the water - smaller
sigils pattering between them. But it's quicksand here
and I can go no further.

      I push aside another curtain
of reeds to find a further stretch of windy water.
Where the reeds grow more thinly - I see Egrets
and Spoonbills - bright backs turned toward the sun.
In a roosting-tree - Spoonbills have already gathered
in the lower branches. Above them cluster Ibises.
Something unseen scares them - they rise a moment -
realise all is clear - and drop back down to water.
A family of Swans - unruffled - glides among Pelicans.

And now a Black-Shouldered Kite is up - half hovering -
half soaring - staring down and searching. She holds
a place in air - dangling for long suspenseful minutes -
rallying - hovering - levelling - head turned downward
toward a spot beyond the reeds - yet sometimes pausing
to check above her shoulder - as if fearing some greater
predator than she might fly behind her. She holds there -
then plummets - hits something by the water. I glimpse
her flying off low behind the reeds.

                         I contemplate the bright
white silence of a Great Egret raising wings and lifting -

my reverie broken by ten Cattle Egrets - ruffed about
with yellow ochres - who come whirling for their roosts.

I want to wait here long into the sunset - but Sandpipers
fly about me peeping - and I know that they are wanting
to be roosting - and this is not my place - so I must leave.

⚹

Back out on Browns Road - a frog lets out a screech.
I find a Tiger Snake at the edge of the wheel ruts -
her victim half-way down her gullet. The fat bulge
makes a quick progression down her body - and she
subsides - divides the grass - leaves for a long time
her lazy embered body out in the road - then draws
it with her. The long grass shivers -
                         sighs -
                                        lies still.

When I reach the meadow - a pair of Swamp Harriers
rises up from under the dock plants right before me.
They have been sitting there - hunkered down among
the weeds - but at my coming - they lift up over rushes
in a ferocious bluster of feathers - their white ringtails
flashing - and fly out in a vicious pincer over Maringup.

Not far from an empty Fox's earth - coiled exquisitely
on the shorter grass - another Snake lies basking.
I draw a startled breath - and she's unbraiding.

I climb up in my Tree to eat a bite and wait for sunset.
A Spoonbill hangs above me - spills air from wings
and plummets sideways - rights herself and skims.
Behind me - Kangaroos crash heavy through the sedges.

Far off in the Creek
               the Coots are diving -
    keen to make the most
                   of failing light -
among them - a smaller bird
         is bobbing
   a Grebe who plops and bobs
                the sun-spilt White.

Three Swans fly above her
               plaintive - piping -
    she's floating closer to me
                  every dive.
A lone Spoonbill is swooping
          right above her -
    the rush of air within
               her feathers' weave -

but still the Grebe is questing -
          now she'll vanish -

    plop up again and swivel
        for the sun.
The Harriers whisk over -
      Crakes a-chatter -
the Harriers spill Terror -
        and are gone.

The little Grebe's still out there
       as the sun goes -
   three Cockatoos are fading
       in the dusk -
and Shelducks - flying homeward
      with a whicker
   through wind that keeps
       their primaries a-whisk.

I look back and the Grebe's
      no longer hunting -
  ripples kiss the Duckweed
       by the shore.
The Kingfisher swoops low
      into the Yandjet -
sunset spills the Creek
       with gentle fire.

Night is falling - the meadow rings with Crickets.
The moon - almost full - is rising - Bats are flying -
and all the way down Browns Road - as before
the Frogs are leaping - but most of these are youngsters -
scarcely more than Tadpoles minus tails.

I turn back beneath the *Melaleucas* - almost weeping.

When I say "Maringup - I love you"

as I'm leaving -
it feels
                    as if I'm speaking
                            to a person.

27 January 2024

Maringup Creek, by kayak
12.56 p.m. to 2.23 p.m.

I had long been agonising over whether to ask permission to take a kayak into Eungedup. In my hypnagogic states before sleep, sometimes I was already out there paddling. Maringup Creek, with its broad stretch of open water, easily accessible from the little shore beside my climbing-Tree where once I saw the Spotted Crake chick, was the obvious place to launch a little voyage, but I had nightmare visions of the birds madly scattering, as they do sometimes when I approach the water from the land, and of paddling out over a temporarily birdless expanse, reproving myself for my selfishness. Perhaps, I have been thinking, I could slip out there slowly, hiding myself as much as possible among reeds, simply wending and waiting to see what transpired.

Last week, I asked the Catchment Committee for permission to take a kayak onto Maringup Creek, and was a little surprised when it was granted. I knew it was a privilege.

The kayak would need to be an inflatable one in order to carry it easily to the open water. My friend wanted to accompany me, to ensure that I'd be safe. I found a kayak – bright orange, unfortunately – with two seats, so that my friend could accompany me on the first voyage of our little craft – inevitably named *Bittern*, in hope. We tested it first on our local harbour, in very shallow water, and today, we have taken it to Maringup.

Beside my climbing-Tree, we spread out the kayak and begin to inflate it. It is a hot day, but I am working in a feverish hurry, desperate to be on the water. Beyond us, the birds on the open water skulk off behind the reeds. We carry *Bittern* down through long grass, underneath the trees where the Kingfisher watches for prey beneath the surface. For the past several weeks, the water levels have been subsiding, so we have to wade out in mud and noisome slush that reaches to the tops of our wellingtons before we can get the kayak to float. We climb in, pole ourselves forward with our oars, and suddenly we're adrift. I stave off a clump of reeds straight ahead of us before we run into it, and gradually, we get the hang of paddling in unison.

I look back to our launching place, memorising what it looks like from the water. Very soon, it is hidden by a bulge in the Yandjet, and we are skirting around the edge of a great, reedy island. In the reedbed to our left, there is a deep, dark sound, like the creaking of a heavy wooden door – a sound we cannot identify. As we round the corner, we encounter three Australasian Grebes afloat just in front of us. To my astonishment and relief, they do not scatter in panic – they hold their positions, watching us calmly. Slowly, they splay ahead of us, decide to dive, and re-emerge further away.

There is a flash of bright blue far across the water. I scan with my binoculars. It is a Blue-Billed Duck – a drake in full breeding splendour, surrounded by several ducks with dark-brown bills. They don't take flight either – in fact, they continue to swim toward us, diving occasionally for food, re-emerging glistening with runnels. My friend has caught my sense of wonder. She notices that the drake's bill and the sky are precisely the same shade of powder blue. It is a colour that I have seen here also in the wings of little Butterflies, and on the upper body of the Sacred Kingfisher.

At last, one by one, the Blue-Bills slip off below the surface, re-emerging behind a thin curtain of reeds, and watching our progress. Musk Ducks too are on the open water beside us – a male is calling – that same watery, plangent plop I have heard so many times from dry land. Out here, it is the language of Maringup – the cool, wet slop of living. A family of Swans arch their necks, holding their heads low down to the water, regarding us calmly.

We paddle down a narrow passage through the reeds. A light wind travels through it, catches us amidships, and forces us to strive at the oars. I reach out once more to stave off reeds with my paddle. A Swamphen stands on top of a half-crushed little island of Yandjet, staring at us quizzically. The wind catches us again, and *Bittern* swivels in the water. We strain to bring her back under control, and simultaneously both of us decide that the wetland doesn't want us to paddle any further.

Gradually, we retrace our course beside the great reedbed, then allow ourselves to be wafted out toward the opposite bank of the creek. I can see the bone-white roosting-trees in the middle of the water toward the wetland's western extremity, fruiting with the long black bodies of resting Cormorants, all their wings closed, their sharp heads snaking toward the sky. The wind buffets again, and we're twirling on the water. It takes some effort to propel ourselves across the open water, back toward our landing place, and I am grateful that on our departure, I turned around to catch a visual impression of what it looked like from the water – how it hid behind that bulge in the reedbed – how its position could be located more easily by looking at the downward curve of the Peppermint woodland behind it.

Quite suddenly, we are out of the wind again, and everything is easier. We slide up across the mud, and I am out of the kayak, pulling it in to harbour. We carry *Bittern* low, so that the cloying mud can be scuffed off in the long grass. Behind us, a large flock of Shelducks eddies in the air and comes in to land on Maringup, their voices loudly whizzing. We pull out plugs, and with a low whistle, *Bittern* is deflating. I too am breathing out – not yet with elation, but relief. Once we were on the water, we and the birds seemed to have a different relationship entirely. We were no longer land animals – potential predators – but something aquatic – albeit something rather ungainly – something to be regarded calmly, and not feared.

The next time I come here with *Bittern*, it will be with many hours to spare. I'll come here on a windless morning, with my lunch, and plenty of sunscreen and fresh water. My voyage will stick closely to the edges of the reeds. I will find reed-screens to hide behind and wait – perhaps even find a way of mooring myself and tying down my paddles – so that I can lapse into the completest silence, watching through my binoculars, waiting until the Blue-Billed Ducks sail toward me of their own accord.

Blue-Billed Ducks are as ungainly on the land as we are on the water. They are hesitant to fly – preferring diving as a means of escaping potential predators – and indeed, during moulting season, they probably can scarcely lift off the water at all. Those wind gusts which left us temporarily disempowered – eddying without volition on the water – were disconcerting and undignified for a moment, but now they fill me with a sudden, soaring joy. Out on the surface, in the Blue-Billed Ducks' wet element, I – a mere land animal – can meet them on their own terms.

I'll be out there -
                     dabbling and aimlessly drifting -
      sometimes swirling
                          in an unexpected wind gust -
out where the Blue-Billed Ducks
                  glide and dive precisely,
     floating in their mastery,
                  living at the
                        apex
                              of their power.

Driving back along Browns Road, Blue-Spotted Hawker Dragonflies hang in the air, regarding us through the windscreen with the great, spotted, compound orbs of their eyes. I must slow right down, so that they stop in air before us and fly on up above us, carrying spatters of that sky-colour in their bodies. Half a tree-height above us, in brown-flecked immature plumage, a Sea Eagle glides – the same individual, I am sure, as the one which cleaved through flocks of waterbirds for the sheer joy of it the last time I visited.

We drive homeward. Behind us, every moment, some awe-inspiring spectacle is unfolding at Eungedup – only for itself – and not for human eyes.

28 January 2024

Near the shed, Northwest Wetland
5.41 p.m. to 7.59 p.m.

All along Lake Saide Road
as I drive toward Eungedup -
Straw-Necked Ibises are stalking
the open fields - probing into soil
with long curved bills at the ends
of leathern heads - prospecting
after worms. They move like herds
across the close-grazed grass -
leaving not a sward untested -
systematic in their hunting.

Off Browns Road - along the causeway
to the shed - my own footprints have left
a trail still visible in the long grass - I step
in the same places - keeping low
and silent behind the reeds.

At the wetland's edge -
Swamphens are sentinels
trampling the foliage to get
a better view - stalking the silt -
ready in an instant to raise alarms
in high-pitched whistling squelches -
or splatter off across the water
in a frenzy. I skulk - stay in hiding.

A Wood Sandpiper finds a perch
in mid-water - turns her long grey back
toward me - tilts her bill to watch
a White-Faced Heron who flies
kink-necked and calling. A Grey Teal
settles in the shallows - loudly quacking.
Black Ducks seem to answer - hoarse
and raucous. Beyond the reeds' next curtain
I count fifty Spoonbills roosting
on the water's muddy margin
great flat spatulas folded neatly
under wings. Every few exhalations -
little flocks of Shelducks gather
somewhere distant. On the grass
beside the water - a pair of Fairywrens
runs about in spurts - pausing to pick
at insects. Soon enough they're joined
by a little flock of others - they feed -
and just as quickly - move on.

Black Cormorants descend. There are ructions
among the Spoonbills. Some fly - but most
sit tight. A reed's height before me - a Black Swan
glides downward without noticing I'm here -
head turned toward the wetland. When she lands -
beyond the reedy curtain - Swans' voices
soon are fluting - gorgeous in their greeting.
Their calling - at near-sunset - is sanguine like
their faces - resonant and bright amid the green.

Five Great Egrets rise at low trajectories -
splicing through the atmosphere - avid spears
of whiteness. The Swamphens have stopped worrying.
A pair of Shelducks whizzes so close I see the white
around their eyes - and suddenly arising in a blaze
of splaying pinions - a Harrier is here - announced
by a clamour of anxious voices. Flying just ahead of her -
another bird of similar size - her mate - I think at first -
until the silhouette resolves itself - a Heron -
lifting up through thermals
                beyond the Harrier
          wheeling one way -
                    then another -
              until both bird-forms
                          are extinguished
    in the pale blaze
        of sunlight -
                the great white orb
                        descending
    two fingers' width
        above the horizon.

Something has flushed
the Spoonbills.
They fly off
in a body -
and seconds later -
everything
has followed.

Great flocks of Shelducks and Grey Teals
are whirling skyward - making for Lake Saide.
The air is flecked with flying shreds of Egrets
like ashes of burnt paper. Only the Swamphens
are staying - and Black Ducks - somewhere afar
hoarsely laughing. The sun - behind a cloud
splits into rays - reappears - bites into
distant dunelands with its white consuming orb -
backlights clouds in salmon. At the precise moment
of its sinking - Swamphens wheeze in chorus -
a family of Swans flutes and gently trumpets -
Ravens call in flight - Cockatoos etch the distance -
and the water comes alive with patterings
and splashes. A Crake lets off her rattles.

I've been kneeling here unmoving for an hour
in obeisance to the wetland - now I stand - shake
the blood back to my legs - fade behind the reeds
and all's at peace.

                I make my way
back toward
Browns Road -
treading in my bootprints -
see the light fading
on the bonelike trunks
of Myrtles -
      look upward -
as flocks of Ibises

        fly roostwards
    from the fields -

and driving off down Lake Saide Road
      I slow to watch
          a Boobook Owl
   who stares back
      at my headlights -
        calmly turns
           and takes to air
     flying noiseless
        into the wide
            and beckoning night.

Bunuru

4 February 2024

*North shore of Maringup Creek, and near the shed,
Northwest Wetland*
2.03 p.m. to 5.20 p.m.

Bunuru is the time of drying. Young birds are fledged and fending for themselves – even the new year's Koolbardies have stopped their chelping. The wetland waters ebb. Frogs and dragonflies are in their second summer generations. White and fragrant flowers, heavy with nectar, burst out on the gum trees. Honeyeaters stun themselves on sunlight and fermentation. Reed Warblers have ceased their singing.

From time immemorial, Noongar people came down here from Porongurup and Koi Kyeunu-ruff, seeking the ocean's bounty – and living off the wetland – place of plenty – and the wetland let them in.

Parts that once were quagmires, or under open water, now are dry enough for walking if you sweep the grass before you with a stick – respect the Tiger Snake – and test the mud by poking before trusting it with your weight. The birds are turning inward – toward what remains of open water. You can stalk behind the reeds where they form the thinnest curtains and, provided you are silent, the birds won't flee – they'll go about their lives unfrightened and never heed you.

There has only been the merest smattering of rain.

Eungedup's waters
>are receding
leaving little silted islands
>every inch of which
is marked by prints
>of Crakes -
their little splaying toes -
>their swiftly plying bills.

Broad muddy shores
>have emerged -
>>neither land
nor water -
>but a noisome slurry
>>over which
the outward journeys of Birds
are marked by tracks
>and runnels
>>in the *Azolla*
like maps of silty deltas.

Beyond my Tree I see
>a Black Duck standing
>>on the silt
her wise handsome eye
>agleam in a mask
of perfect velvet -
but her bill
>is piled and caked with mud
>>which drips and splats
about her as she dibbles.

Then she slips
>	into a smooth broad swirl
>		of *Azolla*.
>	Her long dark wake
>		leaves a lasting trail
>			in the chlorophyll green
>		and rusty scum
>			and the wet sounds
>				of her feeding
>	rise up to my climbing-Tree
>		as I reach a higher
>				branch.

She has taken
>	from walking to swimming
>		in one smooth inscrutable movement.
>			As her bill slides into water
>		it is washed completely
>			emerging mudless.

>		She meanders
>			like a river
>		past the sudden blatant
>			Swamphen's wedge
>				of crimson
>			where it's standing
>				red-stilted
>				on an island.

Wind shapes the edge
   of the *Azolla*
     like a shoreline.

      Beyond it Shelducks
         upend -
  their tail-ends smelted copper.

    Tree Martins scud
      the windswept water
  and by the roosting-trees
    gruff Pelicans are taking shelter
      grumbling.

In many places
  the water is now so shallow
    Black Ducks are standing
      in the middle of open water
  which barely reaches their breasts -
    heads tucked inward
      occasionally preening.

I'd hoped to bring the kayak
  but the wind forbade it -

    now the surface
      is a wind-whipped
    maze
    but the *Azolla* is unmoving -

      a broad flat plain of greenness
          beneath the Peppermints'
                    long shadows.

I wander out into the Northwest Wetland
further than I have ever managed - far beyond
the shed. Here great sheets of water
have evaporated - ebbed - and fresh grass
has colonised the silt. There are tracks
of Kangaroos - etched deep in blackness
and places where the mud cloys to the knees.

I'm walking here on edge - expecting Snakes -
and my wellingtons leave a trail that winds
and falters - changes course and wanders
between the standing sheets of reeds and out
into the open. I see Birds behind the veils
stretching titanium wings -
spreading flawless tails.

All across the wetland
the Black-Shouldered Kite
has her hovering-places predetermined
by fluorescence - her eyes can see
the latrines of Rodents as shimmering lights.

She holds her place against the wind
with rapid flapping - and I think
I hear her chattering. Then at last
she lets go of striving -

holds wings outstretched
and wind assists her drift.

She halts again in air - hovers -
drops suddenly lower as though
the rope of some hidden trapeze
was given play -
>
> then
>
> plummets
>
> straight
>
> down
>
> behind
>
> reeds.

A moment later - she's flying
> at a diagonal -

something in her talons. She brings
them forward - snips the furry morsel
with her mercy-killing bill
> veers -
>
> > disappears.

The trail she leaves in air
lingers in my memory
with its own imagined fluorescence
etched in hypnagogia.

It is like the delta trails
of wildfowl and Rakalis
through *Azolla* - like the map

of my own habitual strayings
                            and restless wendings
                                        through the wetland.

Where she flies - my sense will follow
over shorelines - over shallows
keeping watches - at the edges
over field-drains - over sedges

etching trails - soaring westward -
spilling wind - easing eastward -
never resting - every quarter
is the red-eyed hunter's acre -

and the wind - and the wonder
is Everywhere - I wander -
in the delta of my wendings -
in her plunging - is my Ending.

10 February 2024
Maringup Creek, by kayak
8.54 a.m. to 11:45 a.m.

Yandjet makes bays and inlets. Fish
skip across the surface of the water.
I see the Dragonflies in a different light.
I have been eye to eye with them on land -
but when I am out upon the water - afloat
amid the element of their birthing - sun
catches them with a fresh electricity.

The Black Swans raise alarm calls - but
to my consummate delight - the Spoonbills
high up in their roosting-trees ignore me
even when I row straight past them -
they sit out upon their muddy island
free from intrusions. One of their trees
is not a skeleton - but has sprouted back
to life - tufts of leafy branches thrusting
out of the splintered trunk.

                        I discover
I can moor myself by grasping hold
of reeds. If I grip them in both hands
I do not drift. A Sea Eagle appears -
instantly startling into air a quacking flock
of four Black Ducks. It's the same Eagle
I've been seeing on recent visits -
the plumage still muddy-coloured

up above - but already the spreading tail
gleams bright white every time the Eagle
twists his back upon the sun. He stands
in air - and above him at once I notice
another raptor too high to identify. They wheel
                                                  effortless
                                  turning circles
                         in identical directions
                but their circumferences
       are different.
Sometimes
        at the outer edge of
                her circumference
                        the more distant bird
                              becomes invisible
                                      to me.

A Pied Cormorant scuds across my sight.

I decide I will not leave this spot until
the Sea Eagle decides herself to leave.

I dangle one hand in water. She is circling
                              further off now
                                   still the same
                            tight patterns
              so that if she left a trail
     in air
            the entire sky
                  would be inscribed

                    with childlike
                            scribbles.

She isn't over water any more
        but over land -
                the thin skin of land
                        between Eungedup
                        and the Ocean -

and another raptor is up in front of her -
much smaller - it stoops and loops and
stoops again precipitately - zooms
                        in a parabola
                            over water -
                                    takes a tilt
                        at a Musk Duck
                who slaps desperate wings
        against the surface
raising a frantic
        spectrum of spray -
                then swoops off
                    at a low trajectory.
                        It has all happened
                    so quickly -
        I can't be sure
    of the identity -
            but certainly
                a Falcon -
                        with a Falcon-hooded
                                eye - and talons -

                              a bold talent
                                        for the wildest
                        aerobatics of grace -
                  a wicked sense of eyesight
            and a mind-shuddering
                              propensity
for breaking necks.

I look back
to where the Sea Eagle
      had been circling
            but she is gone -
      she's turned her back
and soared out
over sea.

A Hoary-Headed Grebe dives sequentially
a little further away each time he rises.
A pair of Musk Ducks regards me from
mid-water. The male lifts up on his legs -
shakes the droplets from his body. Together
they continue to quietly glide. A Dragonfly
snaps its wings beside me. Right behind me
a Swamphen clambering through the reeds
comes unexpected on me - squawks and batters.

A Musk Duck swims close by me. Almost
her entire body is submarine - only her head
protrudes above the surface. I can see
a webbed-foot's width of water slipping over

her submerged body slick with air-bubbles.
I see her dip down her head - propel herself -
emerge further - where the wind disturbs
the water. A Spoonbill flies in from the roost -
its eye regards me calmly as it swerves
beside me - two Dragonflies traversing here
in tandem.

I find myself navigating a maze
of clumping reeds and open water.
        A shed feather
     upturned
   on the surface
    is a skiff
       rotating
          in the breeze.

Rounding a corner of a channel through the reeds, I suddenly encounter open water – unintentionally sending up a whirl of birds who spiral up above me, and wheel in air over my shoulder – Cormorants – Black Ducks – Swans. All of them are flying – whirring – crying. I hang my head in sorrow, turn the kayak, and hide myself as quickly as I can behind a reed curtain. Everything settles.

I find myself approaching to the southern shore of Maringup, and come upon a muddy bank no human being can walk, for it is surrounded on all sides by protecting reeds. Every footprint upon it is a bird's or a Rakali's. I keep it that way – let the slow breeze take me.

Grassbirds probe the sunlight with their voices.

I see Reed Warblers inhabiting the outer edges of their worlds
– where the reeds end precipitous in deeper water – and the
Warblers flit and climb about their bases – seeking after insects
– no longer singing – but industrious.

On a tiny muddy island a Spotless Crake is standing, and seems
not to know what to make of me – strange alien being in a
floating orange container – perhaps not even sentient. Why
ever should she care or feel afraid?

Now I float upon a wide pool of *Azolla* - caught
within an inlet in the reeds. From the look of it -
it might be solid - but the water is deeper here
than elsewhere - albeit broth-thick with decay.
I stir the floating matter with my oar - pale hanging
roots of *Azolla* swirl and quiver - over the living
      Cauldron.

Another little inlet
      is reserved solely
           for Red and Blue Damselflies
              all flying tandem
           hovering over slumping
                   vegetation.
Two pairs of them
      have gathered on
           a slanting broken reed.
A third pair
      hovers in and joins them

                    the males clutching higher
            the females
                    almost submerged
                            completely
                                    risking all
                    for egg-laying. I see
                            their abdomens curving.
                                    I see
                            their forewings splaying -
            and when the tandem flies
                    all eight wings
                            hold them suspended
                                    an inch above drowning.
It's a scene
        so delicately poised
                a splash could end it.

A Tau Emerald flies past unhurried - for a moment
he lets go his undercarriage of grasping legs -
flexes them - then stows them back again
beneath the sleekness of his body.

                            A reed leaf
floats on open water. Three more pairs
of Damselflies cling to it. A Swamphen -
noticing me - begins to shriek - I dip
my paddles in slow retreat.

                            Further out
on open water - I see long straight streams

of sunlight piercing to the bottom - churning
up a swirl of tiny organisms - their bodies
transparent - half-way to microscopic - *Daphnia*
and *Cyclops* - *Paramecium* perhaps, with a million
beating cilia - churned up by my paddles -
dabbled into indiscriminately by the bills of ducks -
filtered through lamellae - themselves engulfing
algae - decaying vegetation - plumping up
those bigger bodies - feeding plumes of iridescence.

I look down for a long time into this living
sunlit consommé that keeps it all sustained.

The wind – predicted for midday – begins to stir, and seems to guide me of its own accord back toward my landing. I take its hint and end my morning's voyaging. I row back – and for a while I'm paddling in wet stuff which is neither land nor water, too deep for stepping into. I kneel forward – pole myself through soup. Each time I lift the oar, mud splatters down my arms – over the taut skin of the kayak – and when I take the plunge it sucks about my wellingtons – which pull out with a thluck every step I take – the slick stink rising. *Bittern* smears upon the grass – grimed with slime which engrains beneath my nails as I deflate it. I wipe away the sweat – and something in me is singing.

All the way home the rank smell sets me glowing. My friend sees me pull into the drive – my face red and elated – and though I ache – I'm living, laughing as the kayak, besmeared from bow to stern, is rolled out stinking on the lawn – ready for a dousing.

I get into the shower. A glut of living mud and sunscreen runnels down my limbs –

        sluices

                from my body.

18 February 2024

North shore of Maringup Creek
8.30 a.m. to 11:30 a.m.

On Browns Road a half-grown Joey's grazing -
almost listless - and does not flee
at my approach - but keeps on eating - looks up
at me undaunted. At the corner of one eye
a tick is sucking. He turns tail - takes two leaps
from off the gravel - sits there staring -
ears no higher than the seed-heads of the grasses.

The whole place aches for rain. Mud flats - where
just weeks ago Sandpipers waded knee-deep -
now are plains - all of them evaporated - drained
and everywhere encroaching - a green tide
of windmill grass that quivers in the breeze.

The birds have all retreated to what remains
of open water. I'd hoped to launch my kayak -
but when I reach the shore of Maringup I see
great flocks of Shelducks have shifted here
and I cannot bear to scare them. Last night
my father lent me the old dissecting microscope
he used to show me "water fleas" when I was
only small - so I wade out amid *Azolla* - dip
a jar and bring up a slosh of mud and water -
set up a little laboratory beneath my climbing-Tree
and begin a different kind of watching.

In my parents' family album, there is a particular photograph I am recalling now. The scene is the Stromlo pine forest, near Canberra, 1971. I am two or three years old, carrying my father's fishing net and billycan. The inscription on the back of the photograph says, "Giles on a fishing trip in pine forests near home in Weston, A.C.T.", but there were no fishing trips, in the normal sense of the word, in our family at that time, and the billy was not for fish but for other water creatures. We had a separate billycan for brewing the tea when camping – not because of any fastidiousness, but because my father feared that the detergent used to clean the tea-billy might be injurious to our captures – creatures beneath many another person's notice – tiny lives which must be treated with respect.

The photograph shows me carrying a little brown corduroy bag around my waist. It was handmade by my mother, perhaps on the old treadle Singer machine that she always preferred to her modern electrical one. No doubt it was filled with empty shells of Cicada nymphs, hatched-out gum-moth pupae, and the goggle-eyed cones of *Casuarinas*. I am standing on a wooden bridge which ends, I seem to remember, in a cattle grid, and once when I squatted, bare knees about my head, to look within, a bright green frog looked up at me, imitating my pose.

As I pull the stereo microscope from its case and set it up in the shade of the Peppermints, I recognise myself in this picture. I am still this boy – and I'm feeling the same thrill now.

Just after the photograph was taken, a thick haze of mist swirled over the surface of the river, and whirled in eddies as my father poised the net. The look of anticipation in his eyes was enough to make me tremble from head to toe. Suddenly, decisively, he plunged it into the water, and a moment later, it came up dripping and bulging. A frond of waterweed slimed slowly down the outside of the net as the water sluiced through the fine mesh. Beneath the surface, mud-clouds blossomed.

He was peering into the net now, water cascading over his hands, motioning for me to come closer. I craned my neck to look inside, and yelped with surprise and delight. A stalk-eyed Yabby gazed up at me, its claws waving ineffectually, and unafraid of the pincers, my father reached into the net and pulled the creature out, deftly grasping it by the thorax. It flicked its articulated tail frantically, and the claws gnashed like crocodile jaws as he held it before my delighted eyes, then dropped it back into the water. With a mysterious smile, my father dangled the inverted net inside the can and snapped shut the lid.

Back at home, under this same microscope, a tiny heart was beating beneath my gaze, as a much smaller creature threshed its twiggy appendages. Its eye was black and deep, and I thought I detected a look of desperation within it. I clapped my eye harder to the eyepiece, and my father's hand guided mine to the focus knob. He showed me how to fine-tune the focus until every bristle seemed a mighty spike, and every internal organ in the creature's transparent body could be seen to writhe and pulsate. I discovered that by slightly shifting the focus, I could travel *through* the creature as different layers of internal organs became sharper. He helped me change objectives, and the magnification doubled. I was mesmerised.

"*Daphnia*," he said quietly. "A water-flea." And then he was silent, savouring the moment, watching with his own delight as a child of three discovered a whole new world in a drop of water. As the years passed, he taught me about them all: the strange *Paramecium* who wandered this way and that, like a lost torpedo, guided by a thousand tiny cilia; the grotesque *Amoeba* who swallowed other creatures whole with a bulge of its body, engulfing them in slime; and the strange, stalked *Vorticella*, their mouths shaped like plumbers' plungers fringed with cilia, gaping for food. My whole life seemed absorbed by this world in miniature, and populated by its unearthly monsters. My father's hand guided mine as we drew them in pencil: a father and his son, both filled with the wonder of discovery, as if we were the first scientists in the world.

⚳

I have my back hunched to the water - huddling
over my microscope. Perhaps behind me the Kingfisher
is plucking a thin silver slip of fish from out the water.
Perhaps a Falcon clouts a smaller bird in air - but today
my gaze is downward - Eungedup reveals itself
on a smaller scale. Leaves of *Azolla* are like
snake scales overlapping - tinged pink at the edges.
Beneath them Water Boatmen scud with bulging
eyes - a minute beetle with a high-domed carapace

is climbing amid the floating roots. A *Cyclops*
jerks past in twitches - trailing eggs on paddles
and long sensory appendages. A Nematode worm -
assuming under magnification the proportions
of a serpent - writhes transparent. *Daphnia*
twitch their antlers. A *Paramecium* at low magnification
moves as if by magic. Squeals of Swamphens
are the soundtrack. Aquatic larvae of flies writhe
or leave behind their empty cellophane skins
amid bright green-helixed strands of *Spirogyra*.
Ostracods like minute mussels - some completely
transparent - some pastel green and orange - swimming
in an articulated rush of frantic appendages
open and close their shells - propel themselves
at surprising speeds - pelting into Duckweeds -
ricocheting so desperately about the Petri dish
I hurry to return them back to freedom - wading
out again - pouring all those myriads in a slurry.

Spirogyra

About the central vacuole
chloroplasts entwine
within each segment - crisscrossing
helices of green.

Strand on strand - will replicate
where the Shoveller dabbles -
threads will float - to meet the sun
amid the rising bubbles -

Ostracod

To naked eyes - a swimming Dot -
a Full Stop - with a Will -
a tiny prod - a minor stir -
sets him all awhirl.

Shrimp encased between two shells -
navigates - by touch -
on an impulse - hurries past -
a live - respiring - Twitch -

Cyclops, Paramecium and Water Boatman

She carries more than half her weight
in eggs - in twitching clusters -
they bat away like paddles
between a tuft of whiskers -

she swims in jerks through floating roots -
bowed antennae twitching -
black and beady out the front
her one eye - ever watching.

A male *Cyclops* - unencumbered -
collides with her at speed
and she recoils - as if a spring
propels her - into weed.

A passing *Paramecium*
a fraction of her size
dodges by - oblivious -
undaunted - lacking eyes.

A Water Boatman - crashes on
determined to careen
through everything. His thrashing oars
obliterate - the scene.

Between Lake Saide and Maringup Creek
the Kikuyu Grass has been mown down -
the goats have made short work of all the brambles -
the sedges now are islands in the dry meadow
awaiting inundation. The water in the well
is too low to be visible - out of it erupt festoons
of bright green weeds - when I come near
there are plops of many frogs leaping from
the foliage to water. I let my eyes slip out
of focus - imagine silt and water spreading
over grassland in the winter - the Swamphens
wading - and all about their feet - the *Daphnia*
and *Cyclops*, the Ostracods and *Paramecium* -
where grass grows now - a fleet of teeming
                                                infusoria.

17 March 2024

A new way into the Northwest Wetland, and then the north shore of Maringup Creek

Dryness. The parched sensation that fills my mouth and wakes me a dozen times a night. The persistent soreness of a desiccated throat. The befuddled fumbling in darkness for my half-empty glass on the bedside table. The desperate sipping – holding the water in the forefront of the mouth until the soreness of the dryness begins to abate. The painful swallow which fails to even moisten the dry oesophagus. The sensation of dryness and numbness – yet strangely also of pain – spreading up the tendons of the limbs. The dry sleepless staring into darkness, made tolerable only by the molten honey song of a Magpie outside my bedroom window.

Dryness of Bunuru. Natural dryness for the time of year, but in the previous seasons there was nowhere near enough rain, so this is dryness compounded, amplified – a feedback loop of dryness. Just recently, there was a little smattering of rain, but not enough to stop the gradual vanishing of the slurry of water and living tadpoles from across Browns Road – the dried silts turned to grey-white powder. Deep hexagonal cracks and half-fossilised kangaroo tracks across the waste that once was open water.

Dryness of soul. Evaporation of connection. Work duties, professional obligations. Deadlines, headlines, abject exhaustion. Separation from Eungedup – the dry shock of returning to the human world after the richness of withdrawal. Weekend after weekend I lack the strength to drive there – and I know that in my absence everything is drying. I spend my weekends curled up at home – sequestered from the world. The knowledge that Eungedup's water is evaporating while I am not watching parches my nights.

At an appointment with my specialist, I learn that there is an enzyme in my blood, creatine kinase, which is normally only released during intense physical activity or times of trauma. Because of this, pending another blood test, he tells me that I should refrain from strenuous exercise. Antinuclear antibodies have also shown up in the test – a possible but inconclusive sign of autoimmune disease. My body is a fortress under siege – perhaps besieging itself – the moat is drying up. Looking at the dark rings under my eyes, and observing the cloud of exhaustion that seems to hang over me as I walk into his surgery, he diagnoses without hesitation that I certainly have a sleep disorder, so in April, I will be tested for sleep apnoea. Every day, I crave a replenishment of refreshing sleep, but sleep itself is drying and exhausting. I would cry – but my tears have long turned dry.

༝

Today, at least, I can muster the strength to return to Eungedup. As I am getting my binoculars and mosquito patches out of the back of my car, a neighbouring farmer pulls up beside me under the trees at the north end of Browns Road. He asks me if I am birdwatching, and I tell him that I'm writing a book about the wetland. He is voluble in defence of the farmer who tilled Eungedup for potatoes, telling me that there have always been Bitterns here – he saw one once – and recounting experiences of seeing swans nesting out in the open on the causeways between the potato drills. He predicts, his tone sagacious, that the Wilson Inlet Catchment Committee will have problems with stopping the Yandjet from taking over, but like them, and like me, he knows that the wetland itself plays a vital role in purifying the water that enters the Inlet. He says that a departmental "expert" on biodiversity once tried to tell him that there were no Carnaby's Cockatoos using the site for feeding or nesting. Both he and I have seen them regularly. He is sceptical about "greenies" – he thinks that agriculture and nature were coexisting at Eungedup. Perhaps they were, for a while, if the Bitterns were always here, but I quietly reflect that one farmer is not like another – that as miners and agri-barons approach, the purchase of Eungedup out of the public purse will long be its salvation.

To my delight, he says that he is happy for me to walk through one of his fields to find a hidden path to the wetland. His last remark before driving off is that the chain around the gate is very stiff, and has to be angled in a certain way. He isn't wrong. I open it fairly easily, but it takes me ten minutes to close it behind me. Exhaustion begins to spread already, and the sun is getting hotter. Suddenly, I get the hang of it, and I'm yomping across his field in my wellingtons, drinking half my water at a gulp. I clamber through the barbed wire fence at the bottom of the field in the place he described to me, and find the path very easily. Its sandy way wends uphill and downhill between trees and over sunbaked sand – I am passing over one of the

great sandy banks that surround the north, west and south of
Eungedup, and everything is tinder-dry.

I walk down through Peppermint woodland
dense enough that the boles rise thin and straight -
on a trail worn more by Kangaroos than human beings.
A Raven bursts from the upper branches - flies out
three times toward the wetland - arcs back and returns -
watches from a distant twig. A Grey Fantail plays
gatekeeper - tail splayed in greeting - leaping
from twig to twig. I am surrounded by the alarm-calls
of dozens of birds. From amid the trees I look out
over the wetland - but can see no open water - only
great swathes of reeds and grass rank in alluvial soil.

At the bottom of the hill - down below the Peppermints'
exposed roots - a thin trickle of clear water has awoken
and tinkles over a sandy path marked only by tracks
of Kangaroos. To my right and to my left - opens out
the meadow drain. It has reached its lowest. I stand still
hoping this is the beginning of its refilling -
but I know it isn't. Heavy rain is not predicted until May.

Beyond the meadow drain - the path splits itself
between the Sword Sedges - it is littered all along
with Kangaroos' skeletal remains. And now I'm out
again at the northwesternmost corner of Eungedup -
greeted by a Dragonfly hovering head-high. A small
Blue Butterfly lifts and drops among grasses' dead stems.

I go by Kangaroo's long bone
and stands of sedges - deep
into the Tiger Snake's domain.
Grasshoppers rattle - launch
long bodies - disguised
as grasses - flip invisible
amid the stubble. Seed-fluff
is breaking from the long
brown heads of Yandjet.
At last I see the water -
worn almost threadbare -
a Heron beats away over it -
daub-faced - flint-grey -
trailing yellow legs - emitting
guttural grumblings.
Two Black Swans swim bleakly.

The wetland at its lowest ebb
is like a mystic fasting -
ruminating upon its silts.
Cracks and tracks in mud
cleave deep like scars.

A second meadow drain is teeming with *Gambusia*s.
The tops of their bodies gleam greenish silver -
I stand up from my crouching and -

                          a Peregrine Falcon
            arches out
                  above my head

                  stoops
         behind a line of Peppermints
                           re-emerges -
loops about above the Yandjet -
     soars up once more
              above the trees.

           Her tail
                    splays out like a fan
     then turns streamlined
and with a sudden
              beating of the wings
     she gains velocity -
                  is gone again
beyond the trees.

I think this glimpse is all I'm getting
     but then she's up
           above the reeds again
flying in effortless swirls
     sometimes floating low
         and swooping
              at something -
lifting up and dropping her head
         downward
             in pauses
                  between wingbeats -
her great talons
         clustered in a clump
             ready for unclenching.

She can be right over my head
                one moment -
        and ascending almost to invisibility
                      the next -
    her speed

            astonishes

    as her prey
        must surely die
            astonished.

Now she is a distant
        plunging arrowhead
            of flint
aimed gratuitously
        at nothing
                and she's back above me
                      but higher
catching a swirl
        twisting a gyre
                up in the firmament -
and winds up
        way above open water.
                I see her gather her wings
        against her body
                and stoop
only to pull out of it
                precipitously -

    then catching thermals
                    once again
                              suddenly to plunge
                                    behind reeds.

At ferocious velocity
        she swoops down over the surface
                her talons almost touching it -
    and in an instant sweeps again beyond the trees.

This process is repeated
                at least a dozen times -
    but now she's outstripped me
                far beyond the shed
        and I realise
            all the time
                    she has been airborne
    every other bird was silent.
        I still see her
            whirling
        safely distant
    spilling silent terror
        from her backlit wings.

For long minutes it is as if no bird ever existed, until the calls of Swamphens fill her absence, and just as quickly, two Swamp Harriers also rise and fly along the dwindling lanes of water, scattering a terrified shrapnel of silence.

A place where I watched Shelducks and Egrets is mud-pan now – so dry that I can walk across it. Here I see the open waters' shrinking bodies and gaunt birds leaning into wind – gleaning what they can – and from dry ground right out in the wetland's former centre – I look out to where Grey Teals, Pelicans, Australasian Grebes have congregated – clinging to the deepest stretches – their populations concentrated under remorseless eyes of Raptors. The Black-Shouldered Kite has great swaying green grass meadows to hover over. She sticks to the thin margins of lower turf between the reeds and what once was open water.

Crickets are stridulating where Tadpoles used to swim.

Hanging with no more
      quiver
      than a compass blade
      at twice tree height
      over Rodents' latrines
      the white Kite
      is zeroing her vision.
      A gust of wind
      buffets her side
      twists one wing upward
      but she is not deflected
      a single degree.
           Methodically -
           she quarters
           the edges
           of the wetland

                    with a dozen
                    aerial stakeouts.
                                At the most
                                miraculous times
                                she stands in air
                                perfectly
                                motionless -
                                both wings
                                arced in curves
                                above her body.

                    But this time
                        half-way round her circuit
                    she seems to change her mind
            and makes directly for the tallest
Juniper Myrtle on Browns Road - where she perches
high up in the shade under dusty green leaves
and smoke-grey flowers.
                        I follow her
                                to Browns Road.
                    I look up at her
                            and she looks down on me.
                    We slip into that zone
                            of mutual awareness.
                    She looks straight at me
                            with ruby-angry eyes -
                    turns her head
                            to stare out
                    beyond her back
                            over Lake Saide
                    ignoring me.

Out on the meadow between me and Maringup Creek, dryness creeps like cancer. The weeds around the well are now all dead and shrivelled – gone to seed – collapsed against its concrete – but still when I approach it there are multiple plops of Frogs, the water just beyond human reach, dark with rising coolness – inviting touch.

And up my Tree by Maringup Creek I see the place where many Birds have come to cling to shrinking water:

>   flocks of Sandpipers
>   arrow their ways
>   between reeds
>
>   Pelicans - Cormorants - Swans
>   share the shallow spots
>   standing ankle deep
>   and spreading out
>   their wings
>   to rising
>   wind.
>
>   Spoonbills - Egrets - Shelducks
>   use reedbeds as wind-breaks
>   their bodies reflected
>   in unruffled water.

Others congregate
    in clusters
        at the bases of distant
            roosting-trees
  tucked away
      from predators
        and wind.

A Whistling Kite
    takes long moments
      flying over
    and the Egrets
      stand still and white
        as bleached trunks
      waiting for her passing.

Now Grebes and Teals
    swim out
        to the bill-red melodies
          of Swamphens.

The wind begins
    to buffet the tree around me.
        I will it to bring clouds and rain -
      replenish

    this wild refuge once again.

I wake from reverie -
    a bird-shaped shadow

      darkens my face a moment -
I'm eye to eye with a Harrier
                      right above me.

Branchlets of *Casuarina* fall
catching in crevices - matting themselves
in the tree's armpits and groins - trapping water
when it runs down trunks - mouldering there -
taking years to compost down - layered
with the growing thatch of more recent fallings.

Perhaps the tree even drinks from the spongiform
interiors they create - or in this time of dryness
a tiny runnel finds its way down fissures
in the bark - and trickles away to soil.

Here among the branches' tangle - high as my head -
something has pushed apart the weave
to make a hole - mysterious nest or dwelling -
deeply dark beyond the aperture - where
in felted comfort there is space for curling
and sleeping - in the care of *Casuarina*.

As I return I'm wondering who it is
that lives there - whether that deep interior
where I did not stick my fingers
is lined with fur or feathers - and when I too
curl and writhe - with pain and the electric itch
within my muscles - a mile away from sleep -
eyes glaring into darkness - I shall be drawn

into the holy simplicity
of that far-from-vacant space
where some significant tiny life
sequesters - from the world.

I get back to the car to discover that the farmer has left a package pinned beneath my windscreen wipers. It contains a CD-ROM full of photographs of Swans' nests – great round mounds of fallen reeds – from the days when Eungedup was a potato farm. A handful of printed photographs, with a note saying that I can keep them, show a large flock of Carnaby's Cockatoos perching in the Peppermints, raucous in their defiance of human "expertise".

A faint hope trickles - water down *Casuarina* bark:
wildness - and wetness - will always find a way.

31 March 2024
*The path into the Northwest Wetland,
and then the north shore of Maringup Creek
5.40 p.m. to 7.10 p.m.*

I have forgotten to bring my water bottle with me, so I drop into the little shop at Youngs Siding, just up the road from Eungedup, to buy something to drink whilst I am walking – surprised to find it open on an Easter Sunday evening. I am wearing a bush-hat and a long waterproof riding coat. The shopkeeper takes one look at me, grins and says, "You're dressed hopefully tonight."

The weather forecast said it would rain today, but it turned out to be the merest smattering in the early morning. It is still overcast, and the clouds look laden, but we're used to this by now. I have started calling it "rainstipation" – it tries to rain – almost turns purple with the effort – and predictably fails. It is no surprise that it has done so again today, but the shopkeeper is right: I wore the waterproofs in hope of being caught in a deluge.

The woman who is being served before me says, "People better start praying for rain if they want their avocados next season." As for me, I can live without avocados, if necessary, but I worry for the frogs.

The mineral water I have purchased is supposedly from Mount Franklin in the Brindabellas on the opposite side of Australia – a glorious mountain near to Canberra which I used to visit with my parents whilst camping on the neighbouring Mount Aggie when I was a small child. There, pale green Macleay's Swallowtails used to offer glimpses of themselves on the edge of the dry sclerophyll woodland. Not far away from there, in a place I shall not disclose, there were fantastically rare Corroboree Frogs and Mountain Katydids with bulbous iridescent red and blue abdomens. Now, I am walking the path through the Peppermint woods to the Northwest Wetland, drinking Mount Franklin water – and –

far up the meadow-drain - Moaning Frogs
have begun their mournful calling - even when
the water is at its lowest ebb - the thin clear trickle
I step over widens to the west of me - and there
a small congregation of them is singing hymns
in chorus - their voices distillations of wind
bottled up underground - emissions of earth.
The same Fantail as last time greets me with bows
and splayings of the tail - and I walk out - exactly
at the moment of sunset. Two Kangaroos - down low
on all fours - are grazing - edging forward
with a punting gait at the edge of the dried-up silt.
Another - lying obscured by freshly grown grass
raises a dark head above it - returns my stare -
settles back down - I turn aside before they think
of fleeing. Right at the centre of the wetland - I reach
what used to be an edge of open water - now lake-deep
in sedges - rushes and lush grass - and far off
where the Swans once floated - a massive Kangaroo
stands - charcoal-coloured paws with long black claws
dangling by his stomach. He has been watching me
before I gave him notice - now he turns - launches
the full weight of his body of solid muscle forward

on his longbones - arches his spine - reaches his rhythm -
pounds away across the cushions of tussocked sedges.

The flower-heads of Yandjet
         are disintegrating
    leaving behind
        long brown spikes -
            the ground littered
       with great clumps
           of fallen reed-fluff -
some of them
      trodden in
          by my footsteps - or
by the feet of Kangaroos
      waiting for the rain
          to wake them.

Everything is yellowing.
        Each plant of Yandjet
    has green leaves
       some fading yellow
           toward the tips
      some striated
          yellow and green
split down the midrib -
      others darkening
          into ochres and umbers.
The Sword Sedges
      freshly in flower
          dangle
              with pale yellow anthers.

Shreds of reed-fluff
        hang from trees
                like spiderwebs.

After sunset the Juniper Myrtles
        with boughs
                gently swaying
        have their own whispers -
            wind shushing
                    between
                            fine-toothed leaves -
Myrtle bark -
        creaking
                against itself -
                      the last chips
                          of Birds
                              awaiting sleep -

and more Moaning Frogs
        awakening.

There is a heavy flapping
                of wings against Yandjet
    in the near darkness.
                A Frog lets out
                        protracted squeals.
        I imagine
                an Egret's long spear
    transfixing the Frog -
        wet limbs writhing -
                the death-song fading

                    into silence
        as the light is dying -

and all around the Moaning Frogs
                                    emitting
                        wild and mournful orisons.

Hidden away in the near darkness close to the edge of Maringup Creek I hear a vocal host of Shelducks – their calls layered in distance – knitted into night-time – woven with whistlings of wings and calling crickets stitching up the distance. The beautiful flutings of Black Swans intermingle with bright red stitches of the Swamphens' soprano – and far away I hear more Moaning Frogs breathing out their souls.

Out on the meadow, deep thumpings in darkness let me know I'm not alone. Dimly I notice tall sentinel figures of Kangaroos – their shoulders up above the rushes – leaning against their tails.

Midges congregate in clouds, colliding with my light, so I switch it off and let my eyes accommodate to dark. Their high incessant hums harmonise with the frogs.

I walk back torchless and let the sounds consume me – the leap of something heavy fleeing into undergrowth – a dense ball of fur-wrapped body – a Quenda I think – soft rustlings – creaks and groans of arching trees – and growing fainter – the drawn-out doleful moans of Moaning Frogs mating – or praying perhaps for rain.

Moaning Frogs
Heleioporus eyrei

I've watched them crawling - bleary-eyed -
above the ground - bewildered -
hunched in body - blunt of head -
by human noise - unbothered -

but now they're buried under loam
the woodland fills with moaning -
a pulsing chorus - resonates -
and will not end - 'til morning -

filled with fog - as hollow logs -
moss-growth morphed to sound -
the voice of fungus - widening -
swelling - underground -

choristers whose stalls are roots -
burrowed far from harm
breathing out the Beetle-grub -
the Earwig - Slug - and Worm -

the earth above them caked and parched
as summer works its worst -
they are - groined Underground
in chapels of - the Moist -

Djeran

2 April 2024
At home

The first cool nights of Djeran come so suddenly that the dogs sit wistfully in front of the wood-heater hoping that someone will light it. There is a hint of dew in the early mornings, and the Ants are growing wings. Red flower-buds begin to burst. This is the time when, for Noongar people, the roots of the Yandjet are ready for eating. Just a few days before the season began, there was a big influx of migratory Silvereyes in the garden, joining the ones which had remained resident all year.

I have been booked into a sleep study tonight. It happens at home: do-it-yourself. A brief consultation has turned me into the expert home handyperson on how to wire myself up. Electrodes and their wires coil like snakes, waiting for me inside their plastic case. There is a transparent plastic canula to stick up my nostrils, an oximeter on a wristband, a pair of ECG sensors, a pair of effort bands which go around my chest, and a boot sensor to put on my finger and measure my pulse. I must wipe my skin with alcohol and use abrasive pads on the skin before attaching the electrodes, and everything needs to be secured with extra bits of tape so that nothing falls off during the night. The activity of my brain and heart will be monitored, as well as my breathing and the effort it takes for me to breathe. The system will also record my body position throughout the night, and my oxygen saturation levels.

The setup guide for the sleep study looks complicated, but the instructions are better and clearer than those for modular furniture or the erection of flat-packed garden sheds. There are pictures of cross-sections of a person's head, one with obstructive sleep apnoea, and one labelled "normal". Nothing about this feels normal, but the picture of the upper airway collapsed and closing off the trachea might explain a lot – if it applies to me.

In Djeran, the *Banksia* flowers open, with nectar for the insects, birds and Honey Possums. It was the season when cooler nights caused Noongar people to reinforce their *mia mia*s – or shelters – in preparation for the winter seasons, Makuru and Djilba – making ready for the cold and wind and rain. It brings the slow end of the time of stifling heat.

I am tired of waking feeling stifled – tired of desperate thirst in the small hours of the morning. I clutch at hope – unwind the electrode-headed snakes from inside their plastic box.

2–3 April 2024

At home, overnight

Every one of the electrodes itches as the securing tape shrinks onto my skin. My tinnitus seems many times worse than usual – it scribbles around my head like an irritating cloud of midges. The electrodes behind my ears make it difficult to lie comfortably on my side, so I spend a lot of the time lying rigid on my back as the strange pain – half-itch, half-ache – begins to climb up my fingers. It's as if my arms are hollow, and spiders are crawling gradually up their insides toward my elbows, pausing occasionally to bite down hard on my tendons, or tickle my muscles with their spinnerets and pedipalps.

Some hours later, the spiders seem to have climbed up inside my head, where they are repeatedly poisoning the interior of my skull whilst etching the backs of my eyeballs with the tiny claws on the ends of their legs. I'm not quite sure if I have slept at all or not, but it feels as though dinosaurs might have had time to re-evolve in the time I have been lying awake. I try mentally walking down Browns Road into the wetland to take my mind off my urgent need to sleep – so for a while, the tadpoles are once more swimming about over the track, and the songs of Reed Warblers are melding with the cackles of Crakes. But I can't quite step into one of the reedy chapels to look for a Grassbird – or a Swamp Harrier staring me out from her perch on the *Banksia* – without the distraction of the itching returning, and the entanglement of wires about my chest and running down my leg only serves to amplify the sensation of being victim to a rapidly reproducing colony of spiders.

I decide to try lying on my other side again and thinking of the infusoria under the microscope, since counting transparent *Daphnia* ought at least to be more diverting than counting sheep. This is a mistake. The *Daphnia* assume monstrous proportions, and their twiggy appendages – threshing about and lashing against my mind's eye – only compound the urge to squirm about and dash the electrodes from my body.

By this time, I have drunk nearly all of the water beside my bed to alleviate the dryness in my mouth, and I admit to myself that I need desperately to go to the toilet. I know it is not advisable to check the time when you have a sleep disorder – it only amplifies the anxiety – but I check it anyway on the way out of my bedroom-turned-torture-chamber from a story by Edgar Allan Poe, and find out that it is half-past five in the morning.

Returning to bed, I can think of only one more way of tricking my body into sleeping. There is an episode of the ABC Radio program, *Poetica*, still on the internet a decade after the show was inexplicably and lamentably axed, featuring the poetry of John Anderson. His book, *the forest set out like the night*, helped me to reconnect with Australian landscapes when I returned to live here after eighteen years in England. I am in the habit of playing this episode repeatedly, because the actor's readings of Anderson's poetry are exquisitely gentle. Anderson writes about the sound of wind-breath in *Casuarina* trees, compares the glinting effect of sunlight on Australian foliage to the music of Balinese gamelan, and lets his poetry branch out freely as gum trees branch out against the night sky. He died of blood cancer in 1997, but his poetic voice never grows tired in my ears.

He had a reputation for doing and saying things very slowly, and for catching sleep in snatches during the day, because he had undiagnosed sleep apnoea for twenty years.

I don't quite remember hearing the end of the broadcast – I am just suddenly awake again and gasping and there is silence in the earphones. I pull them out, disentangle them from the electrode wires, drink water, and fall asleep again. I dream that I am on a camp with the children from school. Each of them has brought a pet – and all of these are large insects, but in the course of the camp, they begin to shrink down to normal insect size. We're travelling back to school on the coach and every one of the insect pets has somehow acquired terrible injuries – half-severed legs which prevent them from standing upright. The grasshoppers keep struggling around in circles like compass needles. I am weeping, and steeling myself to bear responsibility for this calamity when the parents pick their children up on our arrival – but the children don't seem to have noticed that there is anything wrong – and I am suddenly awake again and gasping.

Now I am on a rapid roller-coaster of sleeping and waking. The dreams are getting worse, and I am wilfully forgetting them. I'm gasping again and draining the rest of the water, and it is five minutes to eight in the morning. I stagger out of my bedroom, feeling – as I often do – more tired than when I went to bed. I stand haggard in front of the bathroom window – what's left of my hair poking upright at clownish angles – and rip off the electrodes and drop them back into the plastic case. I fill in the form that asks me to chronicle the night's events – less graphically than I have done here – throw that in the case too, and slam shut the lid. I dimly realise that it has hurt a bit – ripping off the electrodes – but it felt like a last-minute release from the web of a giant eight-eyed orb spider, its chelicerae an inch away from channering on my brain.

I drive the plastic box back to the sleep clinic. It and I do not have a good relationship. Two weeks until I get the results. I go back home and lie on my bed again, feeling like a tadpole on a drying road.

5 April 2024
At home

More and more convinced that sleep apnoea is contributing to my fatigue, I recently asked my friend to make a sound recording of me snoring. Today, she plays me the result. It is somewhat unnerving.

The snoring isn't loud, exactly, but there is a whistling intake of breath – like air escaping from a full balloon when the rubber neck is stretched taut. The breathing is tortuous in the extreme – so laboured that listening to it is itself an uncomfortable experience. Then it stops completely, and my friend is asking me if I am awake. I reply, groggily, my heart pounding in my ears.

It makes an odd – distinctly unmusical – addition to my collection of sound recordings of Spotted Crakes, Reed Warblers and Musk Ducks: the dry, rasping struggle for breath – the discordant song of exhaustion.

6 April 2024
At home

All the time I have been visiting Eungedup, I have been engaged in a long process of reorientating my longing. My parents emigrated with me to Australia on an Italian ocean liner when I was one year old, and I grew up in Canberra and Sydney, so Australian landscapes are not alien to me, but in my mid-twenties, by necessity, and because of a deep, unresolved yearning, I found myself drawn to return to England.

I stayed there eighteen years, moving about from the mediaeval city of Durham to a woodland in Buckinghamshire to the Isles of Scilly, eventually settling for seven years in rural Oxfordshire, where I felt I had found something like a spiritual home amid the chalk downs engraved with the Uffington White Horse. I gravitated to the landscape's overt ancientness – the distilled simplicity of the Bronze Age chalk figure itself, the once-marine fossils of sea urchins and brachiopods in the chalk of the Ridgeway, a track across the downs which is itself an ancient monument.

This sense of embeddedness meant that when I had to return to Australia to be nearer to my family, leaving the landscape felt like a spiritual amputation.

Arriving here, close to the south-westernmost tip of Western Australia, I underwent a ten-year struggle to re-adapt. When I tried to write about landscapes here, I felt like an imposter, using privileged, superficial words – on Aboriginal land – to describe places which I knew were beautiful, but whose essence I was not feeling in my bones.

I found that only the most liminal spaces in the Western Australian landscape – its littoral zones – were accessible to me at the level of the heart, and I know exactly what I was implying when I gave the title *Strandings* to the first collection of poems I wrote on Australian soil. I felt like flotsam – like an octopus I found once high up the beach at Binalup, choking on dry air.

After that, for a long time, I returned to writing about Welsh mythology and British landscapes, working from my memory, and charging it with yearning. A violent incident, and the overtly misogynistic response of the authorities toward it, only served to drive me further into this shell. Snow, sleet, freezing fog remained my elements. I did not want to be Australian. Brexit and the reactionary tendencies that accompanied it meant that I did not want to be British either – so I was emotionally stateless, yearning for a renewed sense of place.

It is Eungedup which has begun to turn me around. I knew it on that night at the end of my long service leave when I turned back on Browns Road to tell the wetland that I loved it. It helps, I think, that Eungedup is a place of water – if not tidal, then still subject to the ebb and flow of the seasonal rainfall. The landscapes I have loved have always been shaped by water – whether they are the fossilised deposits of ancient seas, palm-covered granite islands in the midst of the Gulf Stream in the North Atlantic Ocean, or places like Eungedup, where the very distinction between land and water is a questionable one – and the answer to that question varies at different times of the year. Liminal spaces – all of them – but Eungedup is contained and partially divided by old sand dunes which are covered with unmistakably Australian woodland.

My fatigue has given me a broad floodplain of time in which to think this over. The poems of John Anderson have helped me with their sense of stillness, and with their quiet observation of how the bulbous parts of *Banksia* cones which hide the seeds are similar in form to the eyes of birds, or the way gum-leaf shapes are echoed in the forms of parrots. Conversations with local Noongar elders – and their open-hearted acceptance of me in spite of all the pain that ongoing colonialism has sown in their lives, not to mention the terrible damage it has done to their landscapes – have begun a different process of reconciliation within me. Almost a year ago now, I sat with a Noongar elder overlooking the gloriously biodiverse wildlife site, Red Moort, near to Koi Kyeunu-ruff, protected under the ownership of Bush Heritage, as the sun set over the dense woodland of thin-trunked, ancient trees after which the site was named – and walked down the next morning to the trickling watercourse that bisects it and helps to give it life. My drama students were told a Noongar story about the Wagyl serpent and the way human beings were entrusted with the role of being "the Carers of Everything", and in the ensuing months, they created a play that responded to that story. That might have been the beginning of the process – the seeds of my own reconciliation sown within me.

Now, I am reconciled when I kneel down and place my palm against the dark, wet silt of Eungedup and my hand comes away caked with it – my palm and fingers' impressions oozing with wetness amid the prints of Waterbirds. I will do this the next time I am there, and not wipe the mud off my hand until it has dried and caked and cracked. Whatever the findings of the sleep clinic, I know that this growing emotional symbiosis with Eungedup's mud is essential to my healing.

After ten years of feeling stifled, when I go to Eungedup and am in touch with its soily water and its watery soil, I have found a place where I can breathe.

8 April 2024

The path into the Northwest Wetland,
and then the north shore of Maringup Creek
9.05 a.m. to 11.57 a.m.

I have come here this time not so much to write
as to make a map of the Northwest Wetland -
the extent of its beds of Yandjet - now completely dry -
its expanses of bare mud - and what remains
of its standing water at this driest moment - I hope -
of Djeran.

      Descending the sandy path through duneland -
single leaves of next season's orchids are protruding
from the path - newly grown since my last visit -
broad leaves sprouting straight from sandy soil
with pale green midribs skyward pointing - rising
in response to the orisons of the Moaning Frogs.

Prodding the grass before me with a stick - in case
of Snakes - I wander through the wetland looking
for standing water. At its westernmost point
a flock of Tree Martins is hovering over a tiny patch
of standing water no deeper than the lengths of their bills.

I wend between stands of Yandjet toward the shed
then make my way south over former open water.
Swathes of wetland are naked mud over which
fresh grass invades. Vague puddles of wetness persist
in places - but water sufficient to float a Duck or Grebe

is restricted to a long thin lake behind the reedy curtains
beyond the farthest meadow drain. Here the Ducks
float in listless flotillas - disinclined to fly or swim away.
I hatch in the forlorn stretches of standing water
on my map - and from a bank of cloud sufficient rain
falls to damp my paper - then falters - clouds subside
and everything submits to the same relentless sunlight.

Half-way along Browns Road - I climb a Juniper Myrtle
to catch a glimpse of Lake Saide - and look across
to discover not a single patch of standing water -
but far off in its middle, Swallows and Martins
are milling inches above the silt - where a patch
of merest moisture gleams in sunshine - surrounded
on all sides by great expanses of dark grey mud -
Lake Saide's only remaining water driven underground.

Floating in the well - a drowned Kookaburra -
must have leapt in after Frogs - too far down
to save himself - drawn to too much water.
                                        I recoil.

But in the old *Banksia* where the Harrier likes to perch
a single yellow flower-spike is bursting into bloom -
and so too the pair of *Banksias* at the edge of the meadow -
each has a single yellow inflorescence thrusting forth
high up amid the grey-green foliage - fresh forerunners
of the nectar-feast of Djeran.

                    I make my way down
    to the edge of Maringup Creek.

                    With splayed fingers
        I plant my hand
                    in Eungedup mud.

        The waters of Maringup
                    seep up - filling
        the handprint I leave behind.

                    Swamphens see me
        screech and scatter.

                        Grey-black mud
            clots between fingers
                        smears my palm
            with grey-black blessing -

so that when I have climbed my Tree beside Maringup Creek and raise my binoculars to my eyes – the smell of Eungedup mud fills my nostrils. I breathe in and see – far out there – a long thin bank of mud – bisecting what is left of open water. All along it are congregated resting birds – Spoonbills – Pelicans – Shelducks – Black Ducks – Grey and Chestnut Teals – Swamphens. The smaller ducks are hunkered down like stones. The long arc of the mud bank, marked in a curve with the hunched backs of resting ducks, looks like a Noongar fish-trap containing the water at its lowest ebb, the ducks living stones carefully placed, marking that arc in a perfect restful curve – marking it as if they had been quarried elsewhere and carried there by careful hands. A Swamphen – the only bird moving – patrols from resting duck to resting duck, its tail raised to reveal the white underside which flashes across the water. The whiteness of Pelicans' undersides and the tall white forms of Spoonbills are gathered like pale quartz boulders at the edges of the arc. Right at the centre of them: a single Black Swan – raising only once in the silence her beautiful fluting voice – a pale-feathered Raptor suddenly above me – the Birds stones or statues – the mud of Eungedup turned dry and flaking from my hand – and now only stillness –

Legend

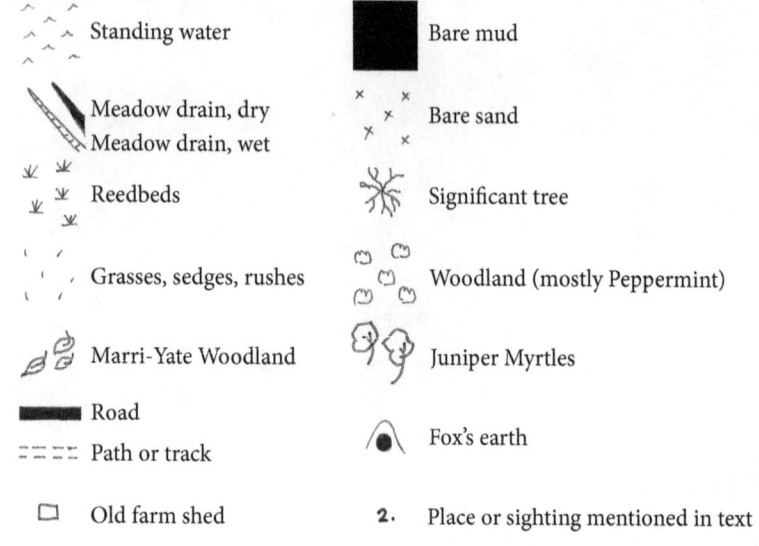

Northwest Wetland in Djeran: Key to places marked on the map

1. Peregrine Falcon sighting
2. Kangaroo skeleton
3. Black-Shouldered Kite's territory
4. Juniper Myrtle trees
5. *Banksia* trees
6. Shallow patch of water where Martins were hovering
7. The path from the farmer's field
8. The farmer's gate

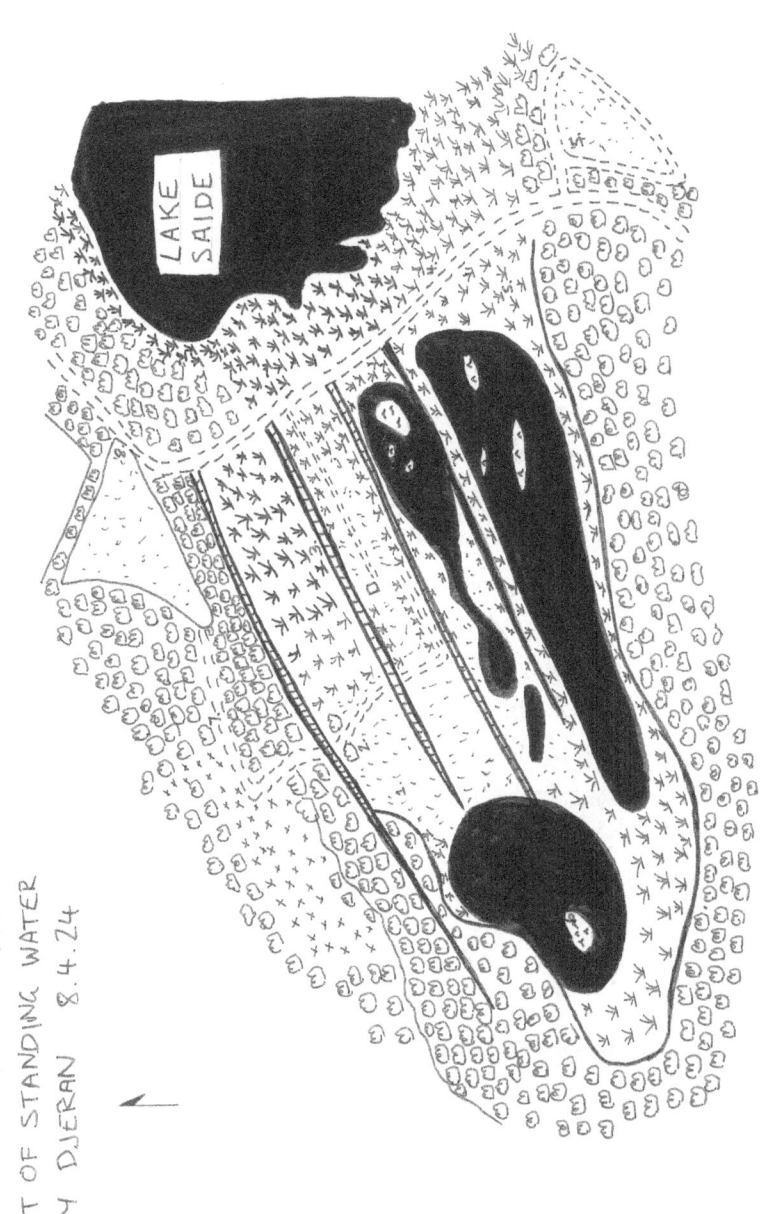

NORTH-WESTERNMOST WETLAND
EXTENT OF STANDING WATER
EARLY DJERAN 8.4.24

10 April 2024
At home

The results of my sleep study arrived yesterday. It shows that in the short time that I slept on the night of the test, I woke up thirty-six times. I underwent twenty-nine obstructive apnoeas, when the airway was physically completely closed, twenty-eight hypopnoeas, when it was partially constricted, and two respiratory effort-related sleep arousals – sudden awakenings after slowed breathing. There are central apnoeas, too – times when I just stopped breathing. The various graphs in the report are strangely mesmerising. I could easily miss sleep, sitting and interpreting them. It means I will need to wear a mask attached to a continuous positive airway pressure (CPAP) machine whenever I sleep, probably in conjunction with a humidifier. I am overjoyed by this news. It may not account for all of my fatigue, but at least something has been diagnosed, and something can be done – on the horizon, a glimmer of a possibility of the end to these dry, exhausting nights.

Overnight, it rained – not an absolute deluge, but enough for the grass to still be wet outside in the middle of the day. Small Songbirds in the garden sip water from the tips of leaves. Now, walking on the beach at Discovery Bay near Kinjarling, I can see a huge bank of dark cloud on the southern and eastern horizons, being carried forward by the wind, and riding before them, Gannets, hurling themselves periodically into the ocean – re-emerging seconds later – ridding their wings of water and scudding on beneath the turmoil in the sky.

Come – long dark bank of cloud. Roll in over Kinjarling and
Eungedup. Release your rain.

I've seen the standing water fade - and vanish -
the Waterbirds all one - where wet remains -
come - deep cloud - unleash - restore - replenish.

Give me breath - and let the wetland flourish -
swamp her - rinse her - fill her meadow-drains.
I've seen the standing water fade - and vanish -

the land - and heart - with nothing left to nourish.
An eerie silence dried the Warbler's strains.
Come - deep cloud - unleash - restore - replenish -

let your moisture spread - like faith - or courage
pulsing through the blood - the lymph - the brains.
I've seen the standing water fade - and vanish:

the rill became a trickle - merest seepage -
no memory of water - save its stains.
Come - deep cloud - unleash - restore - replenish!

Bring the Deluge! Flow! Absorb and nourish!
Green germs! Uncurl within the sleeping grains!
I've seen the standing water fade - and vanish.
Come - deep cloud - unleash - restore - replenish!

14 April 2024

The path into the Northwest Wetland, the north shore of Maringup Creek and westward through woodland between the wetlands 8.40 a.m. to 12.10 p.m.

A mist is rising as I arrive at Eungedup.

As I get down on all fours to pass beneath
the fence where Kangaroos have bent the wire
the grass - dew-covered - wets my knees.
The undergrowth beneath the Peppermints
is tented with gossamer - where in their dozens
Money Spiders have pitched their residences.
A large orb-web - slung from a thistle - stands
in slanting sunlight. Sunlight and Spiders' webs
and the songs of the Koolbardi - Yandjet seeds
hanging - are harbingers of Autumn - first signs
of Djeran - and of rain. Leaves of Slipper Orchids
have lengthened and broadened. Western Rosellas
hang their calls from branches like charms
made of silver or dewdrops glistening.

The meadow-drain runs faster than last time.
Calls of distant Swamphens seem filled
with something fresher - a kind of joy of
expectation. Crake calls rattle - and in the bank -
a fresh-dug rabbit's burrow bears the footprints
of its digger in the wet and fresh-dug soil.

I step again over Kangaroo bones - back
into the wetland. It rings with Crickets.
The sky is full of Swallows - Kangaroos resting
in fresh air and dew-spangled sunlight.
Calls of Silvereyes - Wattlebirds and Ticking Frogs
intermingle. I get wet walking between
the rusty swords of Yandjet. There's no sign yet
of open water growing - yet I feel it - everything
is tipping. Every grass blade drips with dew.
Reed tips - along their knife-edges - carry strings
of crystal. A Kangaroo lurches forward amid
a stand of seeding weeds - turns on hindlegs
to watch me - lollops off easily. Dew-strewn
spiderwebs are slung across grasses - discarded
diadems. Out of the shed bursts a Brown Goshawk
amid an explosion of escaping Swallows - inside it
the guano of birds is strewn. Nightshades grow -
their roots in nitrogen. Pale grey Moths and Blue Butterflies
flutter amid the seeding weeds and *Bolboschoenus*.
A meadow-drain - completely parched on my last visit
is now agleam with wetness. Swamphens
are out there in profusion on the mud - where puddles
have collected. Out over open water - congregations
of Black Ducks and Teals are flying and landing
and in the middle - a pair of Shelducks surface-feeding.
The Teals fill the open with their laughter.
Two Blue-Billed Ducks and a Shoveler weave
amid the multitude. As a Whistling Kite is soaring
she lifts toward the sun and for an instant her back

gleams silver - then her primary feathers are backlit.
She whirls overhead spilling brightness in a trail
behind her - joins her mate above the far west
of the wetland - and the two of them circle
in opposite gyres - winding up the atmosphere -
tilting in recognition of each other where their arcs
coincide - then diverging again - covering
the expanse - rapidly soaring. And then a third
is in the air above me - flying quickly with not
a single wingbeat - descending toward Maringup.
The sun beats down and the sky grows empty.

Amid the grasses and the *Bolboschoenus*
there are trampled and flattened patches
where the Kangaroos have lain. On seed-heads
of the Windmill Grass on the path between
the Yandjet - reed seeds and spiderwebs
intermingle. A pair of Dragonflies skims
above the strewings. One perches a moment
on a long thin strip of Yandjet - green eyes
ogling - then lifts once more - flies swiftly
away from me - turns - returns - looks straight
into my face - and flits aside. I emerge
on Browns Road - boots and gaiters covered
in fluff and seeds of Yandjet.

                      Up the Juniper Myrtle
again - I glimpse Lake Saide - no open water
but a patch of glisten spreading. Hope
grows slowly.

            Beside Maringup Creek
a Western Whistler tests his range of pitches.
Wrens' voices needle. Grasshoppers fill
the dry stems with cringles. Birds' wings
slap the water. Wind lifts the leaves
of Peppermints - lets them down again.
Their tips quiver with after-tremble -
and then stillness. Swamphens speak
to each other in craws and yelps and belches.
Something unknown to me - close by
in the Yandjet - lets out resonant belchings.
I glimpse a patch of mud - a Buff-Banded Rail
streaks across it - chestnut constellation.
A pair of Australasian Grebes are sailing -
between them pass reflections of a long white flock
of Spoonbills.

            Up my Tree by Maringup
I can see the line of open water is advancing -
its leading edge marked by a long thin ribbon
of glisten. Behind a Black Duck - a Grebe
is following closely - diving beneath the wake -
the Duck's feet stirring morsels the Grebe is catching.

From this vantage point - with its narrow view
of swelling open water between the strands of Yandjet
I begin to count the Birds:
                      Black Ducks - Grey Teals -
      hard to distinguish
                from this distance -

        at least a hundred -
              I start to count the Shelducks -
but a Great Egret lands
        among them
              and they scatter.
Seven Spoonbills -
        two Pelicans -
            thirty-seven Shelducks
slowly returning -
            a single Black Swan -
        three Australasian Grebes -
a Silvereye in the tree beside me -
a Grey Heron low flying over water -
        my count disrupted
            by a pair of Harriers
who send the smaller birds
            scudding out
                for open water.
The Harriers' trail through sky
        is marked by dopplers
            of alarm calls.

Whilst I'm up here
    I pay attention
        to the tree
            which gives me vantage.
On one side of its bark
        are two species of Lichens
            crustose - spreading out
                in circles -

fruticose - fuzzing up the branches.
The Peppermint
is one tree
with nine thick trunks
and other spindly ones
growing to replace them.
Another trunk
against which I have leaned
to steady my binoculars
every time I've been here
is long-dead and barkless -
fallen - trapped amid
the living branches.

Spotless Crakes
haunt the edges of the Yandjet -
dark little ghost-shadows
which evaporate
when I look at them.

And just when I think of leaving
two Black-Fronted Dotterels
appear on the waterline
picking away at mud -
and as I watch through my binoculars
the shadow of something
splits and scatters them.
I turn aside to see it
and catch with my eyes
a Hobby whisking eastwards -

                    dark-hooded streak
                            of death and chestnut -
                                    talons clenched.

Black-Fronted Dotterel
Charadrius melanops

Other Waders clung to coasts -
flew oceans every winter -
wayward Dotterels coursed inland
up rivers - seeking water -

scratched their nests on creek beds where
their eggs would pass - for pebbles -
eked out an existence
when wetlands dried - to puddles -

adapted to Australian dearth
persisting through the Drought -
vermilion bibbed and billed with black -
burnt eyelid - smirchless throat -

a flash amid the Drab of Bush -
beneath a rainless sky -
a water-glyph on sudden wings -
a fleeting - pinking - cry

a glimpse beyond the Peppermints -
a brightness here - then gone -
stirred by swooping shadows
or rumourings - of rain -

☽

On the path through the woodland
between the wetlands - I walk further
than I have ever walked. There are lifetimes
of discoveries to be made in this place.
I know that in my comings and goings -
circumscribed by fatigue - I have only
scratched the surface - yet my feet are gripped
by this sandy ground marked by trails
of Lizards and Kangaroo droppings -
frizzled remains of Peppermint leaves -
the long dark back and tail of the Roo
who takes the trail before me - hemmed in
by Sword Sedges - by the territories
of the Grey Fantails - by the overhead
whirling-grounds of Birds of Prey.
I climb this trail - past spiky *Acacias* -
as it winds snakelike over dunes held together
by the roots of grasses - rushes - Peppermints -
Kangaroo Paws - low-growing *Casuarinas*
bending over rustles of Snakes in undergrowth -

and I come
out on a high rise
      on the far western end
           of both wetlands.
   The hills where the lime mine
hides before me -

the trail
        snaking off
                into distance.

I retrace my steps.
        I have only started noticing
                what might be noticed here.

※

Last impressions:

Passing clatter of Dragonflies' wings.

Empty pupa case of Emperor Gum Moth
light as moth-wing - hard as bark.

Parallel tracks of something leaping on sand.

Bulbous lignotuber of Peppermint
broken away - rolled out on the trail.

Spike-leaved insect galls on low-growing bushes
whose twigs - dead at the ends - are homes
for lichens.

Peppermint seedlings growing amid roots
of their parent trees - the ongoing succession
of woodland.

Calls of crakes filtering through
wrist-thin trunks where Peppermints grow densest.

Ropes of *Hardenbergia* hawsering the branches -
pulled taut where a tree has fallen.

Glimpse of Maringup between trees -
blue oasis sustained by blue sky and birdsong.

Grey Fantail swivelling upside down
on tall grey trunk of Peppermint.

Predatory Wasp with brick-red abdomen
hunting amid spent leaves on the sand.

Twigs sticking up amid dry grasses
on an open knoll - Dragonfly perches.

Home of unidentified Mammal - amid
the branchlets of *Casuarina* - mystery
I no longer wish to solve.

Eungedup herself must keep her secrets.
Eungedup must choose which secrets to divulge.
Eungedup must hold some close - keep them
protected. The boughs of Peppermints
at Eungedup bend over to enclose them.
The songs of Birds at Eungedup weave
a fabric to hide them. The trails of Snakes
at Eungedup are a basket to cradle them.

The seeds of sedges at Eungedup
are the future growth to obscure them.

Eungedup is not mine.

Eungedup is not yours.

But as I stand behind the many boles of Peppermint
outside the Yandjet chapel overlooking the *Banksia*
at the edge of the wetland - and a Harrier rears up -
pale ringtail flashing - curving outwards over Yandjet -
I feel myself owned
by Eungedup.

        The fabric of the buzz
of flies - the sudden rush of multitudes of birds' wings -
the song-skeins of Ravens - are weaving me in - making
me part of the tapestry - with no more significance
than the floating seeds of Yandjet that surround me
or the lone Dragonfly who flashes amidst them.

Somehow - now - I am surrendered
to Eungedup's seasonal tides - I dried
as Eungedup dried - and as the hope
of replenishment spreads over Eungedup
I hope
    to be
        replenished.

I walk back down Browns Road
and see a Songbird trailing in its claws
a long thin strip of Yandjet.

A bird has started singing -
I think it is a Warbler.

At the end of Browns Road
I turn back toward Eungedup
and find I am crying.

25 April 2024
At home

I have learnt from two nights of using a CPAP machine that sleeping without one is a slow-parching poison to me. Every time I have stopped breathing in my sleep, my body has been deprived of oxygen. I have awoken in the mornings – and several times a night – feeling that sleep is not refreshment, but an ordeal.

The CPAP machine is going to take some getting used to. I have to strap the mask quite tightly to my face to get a sufficient seal so that air doesn't leak out the sides and reduce the pressure that keeps my airway open. When I switch the machine on, the air pressure is quite mild, but when it detects that I have fallen asleep, it intensifies. Sometimes this wakes me up again straight away – other times, I sleep through it into refreshment. I still don't quite have the humidifier at the right setting – I wake up after a couple of hours with a parched mouth and throat.

But twice now in the mornings, I have had no existential crisis about how I am going to get through the day. I still feel tired, but not remorselessly so to the point of speechless tears. There are still possible warning signs in my blood tests to be investigated – I am under no illusion that correcting my sleep apnoea will be the complete end of my chronic fatigue – but the edge of suppressed panic has disappeared from my waking, and for the first time in years, I got through a day at school yesterday without having to fight that compulsion to lie down on the grass.

The sound of the rushing air from the machine makes it hard for me to hear what the weather is like outside, but there have been more and more rain clouds. Replenishment is in the air. News has recently broken, too, that our Federal Minister for the Environment has made a decision, in response to enormous public pressure from all over Australia, not to approve a "development" that would have destroyed wetlands at Toondah Harbour in Queensland, on the opposite side of the country. Toondah is home to large numbers of endangered migratory waders, including Eastern Curlews. The battle to save it has taken years – but it has succeeded. Over here, Eungedup too is safe from human depredations, and evidence of the efforts to restore it is already visible. The world is in a mass extinction crisis, but people who care *are* succeeding in saving some of our most precious wildernesses, and here in the south-west of Western Australia, the Gondwana Link is actively restoring native vegetation in a broad swathe across the country, connecting what was formerly fragmented and isolated. It is more than just a dream that Eungedup may one day be a part of a spreading wild mosaic.

In the midst of this replenishment, I lie in bed, masked and relaxed, and the borders of my sleep are touched by visions of the waters of Djeran returning to Eungedup – filling the mud-pans, reviving the thirsty Yandjet, reeds and sedges, spilling out over Browns Road, pooling and broadening in the middle of parched Lake Saide, inviting back more frogs in time for breeding, beckoning the wading birds, providing lush hunting places at the edge of the water for Tiger Snakes preparing for semi-hibernation, extending the shallows back from the forlorn remnants of open water, flushing the fish – the Mosquitofish and Native Minnows – back in over the silt – back among the reeds where the Bittern is standing – swaying gently in rhythm with the wind-caught Yandjet – his piercing eyes waiting for the flit of fish tails at the bases of the stems – his sudden stabbing and gobbling movement – his inscrutable return to stasis – stilling – digesting – brewing the deep resonant Bittern boom within his sleek, striated body as he gazes skywards – to the stormclouds and the rain.

I hover at the borders of sleep as the Black-Shouldered Kite hovers over Yandjet. Wakefulness is spilling from my wings. I am held gently aloft – yet losing altitude in a slow parabola – down to reedy ground where wetness creeps –

> renewing.

25 May 2024
Browns Road
2.30 p.m.

On our way home from a shopping trip in Denmark, my friend suggests we drop in on Eungedup. To our astonishment, all across the wetland, drifts of buoyant white fluff are swirling. The wind has caught the Yandjet seeds – thick as snowflakes in a blizzard – lifting them skyward.

They whirl about the reed leaves -
wrap themselves around grass stems -
work their ways into the fabric
of our clothes. They nestle in our hair.

Some are carried on the wind to where
distant mud lies exposed alongside water -
nestling there - resting - settling in. I look up
ebullient and the wind - awhirl with seeds -

sweeps Eungedup upward - to the World.

                                          Rain is coming.

List of Species

Only species observed by me at Eungedup, their unquestionable tracks and signs, or species observed by researchers during the time of my visits to Eungedup are included in this list. It is, therefore, far from being a comprehensive catalogue of the biodiversity of the wetlands but is a fair representation of what might be encountered in the space of a season. Although some introduced vertebrate species are listed because of their environmental significance, invasive plant species have not been included.

BIRDS

Bittern, Australasian (*Botaurus poiciloptilus*)
Cockatoo, Carnaby's (*Zanda latirostris*)
Cockatoo, Forest Red-Tailed Black (*Calyptorhynchus banksii naso*)
Coot, Eurasian (*Fulica atra*)
Cormorant, Great (*Phalacrocorax carbo*)
Cormorant, Little Black (*Phalacrocorax sulcirostris*)
Cormorant, Little Pied (*Microcarbo melanoleucos*)
Crake, Spotted (*Porzana fluminea*)
Crake, Spotless (*Zapornia tabuensis*)
Dotterel, Black-Fronted (*Charadrius melanops*)
Duck, Australasian Shoveler (*Spatula rhynchotis*)
Duck, Australian Wood (*Chenonetta jubata*)
Duck, Blue-Billed (*Oxyura australis*)
Duck, Chestnut Teal (*Anas castanea*)
Duck, Grey Teal (*Anas gracilis*)
Duck, Musk (*Biziura lobata*)
Duck, Pacific Black (*Anas superciliosa*)

Eagle, Wedge-Tailed (*Aquila audax*)
Egret, Western Cattle (*Ardea ibis*)
Egret, Great (*Ardea alba*)
Fairywren, Red-Winged (*Malurus elegans*)
Fairywren, Splendid (*Malurus splendens*)
Falcon, Brown (*Falco berigora*)
Falcon, Peregrine (*Falco peregrinus*)
Fantail, Grey (*Rhipidura albiscapa*)
Firetail, Red-Eared (*Stagonopleura oculata*)
Goshawk, Brown (*Accipiter fasciatus*)
Grassbird, Little (*Poodytes gramineus*)
Grebe, Australasian (*Tachybaptus novaehollandiae*)
Grebe, Hoary-Headed (*Poliocephalus poliocephalus*)
Harrier, Swamp (*Circus approximans*)
Heron, White-Faced (*Egretta novaehollandiae*)
Heron, White-Necked (*Ardea pacifica*)
Hobby, Australian (*Falco longipennis*)
Ibis, Australian White, or Sacred (*Threskiornis molucca*)
Ibis, Straw-Necked (*Threskiornis spinicollis*)
Kingfisher, Sacred (*Todiramphus sanctus*)
Kite, Black-Shouldered (*Elanus axillaris*)
Kite, Whistling (*Haliastur sphenurus*)
Kookaburra, Laughing (*Dacelo novaeguineae*)
Martin, Tree (*Petrochelidon nigricans*)
Magpie, Australian (*Gymnorhina tibicen*) (Noongar: Koolbardi)
Moorhen, Dusky (*Gallinula tenebrosa*)
Owl, Australian Boobook (*Ninox boobook*)
Parrot, Australian Ringneck (*Barnardius zonarius*) (Noongar: Meelya)
Parrot, Red-Capped (*Purpureicephalus spurius*)
Pelican, Australian (*Pelecanus conspicillatus*)

Rail, Buff-Banded (*Hypotaenidia philippensis*)
Raven, Australian (*Corvus coronoides*)
Reed Warbler, Australian (*Acrocephalus australis*)
Rosella, Western (*Platycercus icterotis*)
Sandpiper, Sharp-Tailed (*Calidris acuminata*)
Sandpiper, Wood (*Tringa glareola*)
Sea Eagle, White-Bellied (*Haliaeetus leucogaster*)
Shelduck, Australian (*Tadorna tadornoides*)
Silvereye (*Zosterops lateralis*)
Spinebill, Western (*Acanthorhynchus superciliosus*)
Spoonbill, Yellow-Billed (*Platalea flavipes*)
Swallow, Welcome (*Hirundo neoxena*)
Swamphen, Australasian (*Porphyrio melanotus*)
Swan, Black (*Cygnus atratus*)
Thornbill, Inland (*Acanthiza apicalis*)
Wattlebird, Western (*Anthochaera lunulata*)
Whistler, Western (*Pachycephala fuliginosa*)

MAMMALS
Antechinus, Yellow-Footed (*Antechinus flavipes*)
Bandicoot, Southern Brown (*Isoodon obesulus*) (Noongar: Quenda)
Bats (species not determined)
Fox, Red (*Vulpes vulpes*)
Kangaroo, Western Grey (*Macropus fuliginosus*) (Roo)
Rakali (*Hydromys chrysogaster*)

INSECTS

Cicada, Tick-Tock (*Physeema quadricincta*)

Beetle, Lycid (*Porrostoma* sp.)

Butterfly, Common Brown (*Heteronympha merope*)

Butterfly, Common Grass Blue (*Zizina labradus*)

Butterfly, Grass-Dart (*Taractrocera* sp.)

Butterfly, Australian Painted Lady, (*Vanessa kershawi*)

Butterfly, Western Xenica (*Geitoneura minyas*)

Damselfly, Aurora Bluetail (*Ischnura aurora*)

Damselfly, Blue Ringtail (*Austrolestes annulosus*)

Damselfly, Red and Blue (*Xanthagrion erythroneurum*)

Damselfly, Slender Ringtail (*Austrolestes analis*)

Dragonfly, Blue Skimmer (*Orthetrum caledonicum*)

Dragonfly, Blue-Spotted Hawker (*Adversaeschna brevistyla*)

Dragonfly, Scarlet Percher (*Diplacodes haematodes*)

Dragonfly, Tau Emerald (*Hemicordulia tau*)

Fly, Flower (*Miltinus* sp.)

Fly, Fruit (*Euleia* sp.)

Grasshopper (*Austroicetes cruciata*)

Grasshopper, Gumleaf (*Goniaea australasiae* sp.)

Mosquito (*Aedes* sp.)

Moth, Emperor Gum (*Opodiphthera eucalypti*)

Moth, Golden Grass Carpet (*Anachloris subochraria*)

Moth, Sun (*Synemon* sp.)

Wasp, Black Mud-Dauber (*Sceliphron* sp.)

Wasp, Sand (*Bembix* sp.)

Water Boatman (Corixidae)

SPIDERS
Crab Spider (*Thomisus* sp.)
Garden Orb-Weaver (*Hortophora transmarina*)
Jewel Spider (*Austracantha minax*)
Money Spider (Linyphiidae)
Wolf Spider (*Kangarosa* sp.)

AMPHIBIANS
Moaning Frog (*Heleioporus eyrei*)
Motorbike Frog (*Litoria moorei*)
Rattling Froglet (*Crinia glauerti*)
Slender Tree Frog (*Litoria adelaidensis*)
Ticking Frog (*Geocrinia leai*)
Western Banjo Frog (*Limnodynastes dorsalis*)

REPTILES
Dugite (*Pseudonaja affinis*)
Tiger Snake (*Notechis scutatus*)

FISHES
Bluespot Goby (*Pseudogobius olorum*)
Western Minnow (*Galaxias occidentalis*)
Western Mosquitofish (*Gambusia affinis*)

OTHER AQUATIC INVERTEBRATES
Cyclops sp.
Daphnia sp.
Nematodes
Paramecium sp.
Ostracods

PLANTS

Acacia (various species)
Banksia, Swamp (*Banksia littoralis*)
Bracken Fern (*Pteridium esculentum*)
Duckweed (*Lemna* sp.)
Fern, Mosquito (*Azolla* sp.)
Hardenbergia (*Hardenbergia* sp.)
Hibbertia (*Hibbertia* sp.)
Juniper Myrtle (*Taxandria juniperina*)
Karri (*Eucalyptus diversicolor*)
Marri (*Corymbia calophylla*)
Orchid, Slipper (*Cryptostylis ovata*)
Peppermint, Willow (*Agonis flexuosa*)
Paperbark, Swamp (*Melaleuca rhaphiophylla*)
Rush, Great Soft (*Juncus pallidus*)
Rush, Jointed (*Baumea articulata*)
Rush, Marsh Club (*Bolboschoenus caldwellii*)
Sedge, Coast Sword (*Lepidosperma gladiatum*)
Sheoak (*Casuarina* sp.)
Water Silk (*Spirogyra* sp.)
Reedmace (*Typha orientalis*) (Noongar: Yandjet)
Yate (*Eucalyptus cornuta*)

Acknowledgements

I am grateful to:

Shaun Ossinger, and the Wilson Inlet Catchment Committee, for granting me unlimited access to the Eungedup wetlands when they were closed to the public, and for working tirelessly for the preservation and enhancement of this sensationally beautiful wild space.

Georgia Richter of Fremantle Press, for her meticulousness, sensitivity and encouragement whilst this work was undergoing the editorial process.

Naama Grey-Smith, for helping me to keep my use of scientific names up to date with changes in taxonomy.

Brad Kneebone, for sharing generously from the deep wellspring of his love for – and knowledge and experience of – Eungedup.

Tim Gamblin, for showing me where the Rakalis hang out.

Mark Parre, for spreading quiet wisdom and an infectious enthusiasm for seeds.

Simon Smale, himself an utterly inspired rescuer of wild spaces, for the notion that although it has Spotless Crakes, Eungedup is not a crakeless spot.

Claire Harding, for sharing her expertise on an early walk around Eungedup, for enhancing my understanding of how

Typha comes to dominate a wetland landscape, and for coming up with the idea about the kayak. Cole, her son, for braving snakes and enthusing over frogs.

Kayang Carol Pettersen, for wisdom on the Noongar seasons, and for conversations during camps at Red Moort nature reserve which helped me to walk her people's soil with reverence and awe.

The leadership of Great Southern Grammar School, for granting my long service leave when I most sorely needed it, and the staff of the English Department, for whom the idea that every working building should have a turret, designed to cater for the sudden urge to sleep, is a regular conversation. The late and much-missed Penny Leiper, for a shared love of Emily Dickinson's poetry, and so much more.

My mother and my father, Mary and Leslie Watson, for the upbringing which not only taught me how to observe nature, but how to give it room to let it heal me. As ever, my mother also gave me invaluable help with proofreading this text.

Warren Lilford, photographer, for publicity photographs among the Peppermints.

Simone Keane, for endless, unflinching support, for encouraging me to seek a publisher for *Eungedup*, and for helping me in so many ways to live with chronic fatigue and yet still find inspiration.

The wild things of Eungedup, who gave this project life.

↯

The opening poem 'Bittern' was first published in *Into the Wetlands*, The Wetlands Centre Cockburn, WA Poets Publishing, 2023, and is reproduced here with revisions.

The lyric, 'My Darkness Overturned', was first published in *Creatrix*, no. 62, September 2023.

The quotation from Vitruvius is from his *The Ten Books of Architecture*, translated by Morris Hicky Morgan, Harvard University Press, 1914.

The passage expressing fear of miasma arising from the wetlands of Perth is from *The Inquirer*, Wednesday August 20, 1873, p. 2, trove.nla.gov.au/newspaper/article/65931475.

About the Author

Born in England, Giles Watson migrated to Australia at the age of one, grew up in Canberra, and returned to live in Britain for eighteen years. There, he became fascinated with ancient landscapes, writing prolifically in response. In 2013, he returned to Australia, settling in Kinjarling (Albany), Western Australia. He has a long-standing interest in natural history, mediaeval texts, folklore and mythology, and has worked as a volunteer in wildlife rehabilitation, specialising in orphaned and injured owls. Giles is the author of a large body of poetic work, both self-published and in literary journals, a book of essays on the folklore of natural history, *A Witch's Natural History* (Troy Books), and the novel that inspired *Mimma: A Musical of War and Friendship*. He is the editor of *Ten Poems About Butterflies* (Candlestick Press), and has written songs with singer-songwriter Simone Keane. He teaches English, literature and drama, and lives in Kinjarling (Albany), WA.

www.ingramcontent.com/pod-product-compliance
Lightning Source LLC
Chambersburg PA
CBHW021146160426
43194CB00007B/701